W9-AVL-338

Frederick Douglass

FOR KIDS

His Life with 21 Activities

Copyright © 2012 by Nancy I. Sanders
First edition
Published by Chicago Review Press, Incorporated
814 North Franklin Street
Chicago, Illinois 60610
ISBN 978-1-56976-717-7

Library of Congress Cataloging-in-Publication Data

Sanders, Nancy I.
Frederick Douglass for kids : his life and times with 21 activities / Nancy I. Sanders.
p. cm.
ISBN 978-1-56976-717-7 (pbk.)
1. Douglass, Frederick, 1818–1895—Juvenile literature. 2. Abolitionists—United States—Biography—Juvenile literature. 3. African American abolitionists—Biography—Juvenile literature. 4. Antislavery movements—United States—History—19th century—Juvenile literature. 5. Douglass, Frederick, 1818-1895—Study and teaching—Activity programs. 6. Antislavery movements—United States—Study and teaching—Activity programs. I. Title.

E449.D75S25 2012
973.8092—dc23
[B]

2011050092

Cover and interior design: Sarah Olson
Cover photographs: Frederick Douglass, courtesy University of North Carolina Chapel Hill; Colonel Lloyd's planta-
    tion, courtesy Frederick Douglass–Isaac Myers Maritime Park; "The 54th Massachusetts regiment, under the
    leadership of Colonel Shaw," courtesy Library of Congress, LC-DIG-highsm-09903; Lewis Douglass, courtesy
    Moorland-Spingarn Research Center, Howard University; "Frederick Douglass appealing to President Lincoln
    and his cabinet," courtesy Library of Congress, LC-DIG-highsm-09902
Interior illustrations: Mark Bazuik

Printed in the United States of America
5 4 3 2 1

God bless our native land,
Land of the newly free,
Oh may she ever stand
For truth and liberty.

—from "God Bless Our Native Land"
by Frances Ellen Watkins Harper

～Acknowledgments～

It takes a village to raise a child, and it takes a nation to write a book of this scope and influence. I want to thank the countless men and women who from our nation's earliest history have made a stand for freedom. During the Revolutionary Era, Richard Allen, founder of Bethel A.M.E. Church in Philadelphia and first bishop of the African Methodist Episcopal Church, forged a path for others to follow. His friends and fellow leaders of America's free black communities included giants such as James Forten, Absalom Jones, and Prince Hall. They stood up for equal rights while always fighting to bring an end to slavery. They were followed by a generation of abolitionists both black and white who paved the way for Frederick Douglass to step forward and carry the torch for freedom.

A heart full of gratitude goes out to Douglass biographers such as James Gregory, Frederic Holland, and Charles Chesnutt; Civil War historians such as George Washington Williams and William Wells Brown; along with Benjamin Quarles, Philip S. Foner, Yuval Taylor, and Henry Louis Gates Jr., whose books taught me so much about Frederick Douglass, his world, and our nation's history during the Civil War years.

I want to thank the men and women in our nation's National Park Service who helped guide me on my search to learn more about this great man. Thank you Braden Paynter, Cathy Ingram, Joan Bacharach,

and Amber Dumler. Also many thanks go to the individuals at libraries, universities, and historical societies who so graciously assisted me in acquiring images for this book: Chris Rowsom, Larry Naukam, Betty Spring, Michael Millner, Karen Shafts, Joellen Elbashir, Marie Henke, Beth Hansen, and Peter Berg. I would also like to thank the Tilghman family at Wye house as well as Claire Marziotti. Everyone's generous spirit in sharing images for this project was greatly appreciated.

Thanks go to everyone at Chicago Review Press who worked so hard to bring this book to life. Thank you Jerome Pohlen for all your help and guidance, as well as Cynthia Sherry and Yuval Taylor for your advice and expertise. Special gratitude goes to Michelle Schoob, Sarah Olson, Mary Kravenas, and Josh Williams, who helped launch this book into the world. Deep appreciation is also felt for my wonderful agent, Ronnie Herman, who inspires and guides me along my writing journey.

And I'm especially grateful to my dear husband Jeff, whose committed faith, enthusiasm for our nation's history, and interest in this project helped beyond measure. Thank you to our son Dan and your lovely fiancée Shirley for your loving support and encouragement. And thanks to our son Ben for traveling the East Coast with Jeff and me from Maryland's Eastern Shore to Boston and New Bedford as we took photographs of the streets Frederick Douglass walked and homes he lived in.

CONTENTS

TIME LINE

1817/1818 Frederick Augustus Washington Bailey is born in February, a slave on Maryland's Eastern Shore

1826 Is sent to live in Baltimore as house slave for Hugh Auld family

1836 Makes first attempt to escape, but fails

1838 Escapes from slavery, marries Anna Murray, and changes name to Douglass

1841 Speaks at antislavery convention in Nantucket, Massachusetts, and is hired as antislavery speaker

1842 Defends George Latimer case

1843 Embarks on a "Hundred Conventions" tour

1845 Publishes first autobiography, *Narrative of the Life of Frederick Douglass*

1845 Sails to England to escape capture by slave hunters

Anna Murray Douglass

Harriet Beecher Stowe

1846 English friends raise money to purchase freedom

1847 Returns to United States and begins publication of the *North Star*

1847 Meets with fiery abolitionist John Brown

1848 Speaks at Women's Rights Convention at Seneca Falls, New York

1851 Splits with William Lloyd Garrison over opinions on the constitution and how to end slavery

1852 Delivers famous speech, "What to the Slave is the Fourth of July?"

1852 Is active as leader with Liberty Party convention and Free Soil Party

1853 Accepts invitation to visit Harriet Beecher Stowe

1857 Lectures on the Dred Scott decision

1859 Flees to England after John Brown's raid on Harpers Ferry

1860 Returns to America and mourns death of youngest daughter, Annie

1861 Urges the Union to emancipate the slave and raise black troops at outbreak of Civil War

1863 Celebrates at Tremont Temple on January 1 when Lincoln issues Emancipation Proclamation

1863 Recruits black troops; sons Lewis and Charles are first to enlist in New York

1863 Visits White House to ask Lincoln for equal treatment of black troops

1863 Ends publication of newspapers after 15 years

1864 Lincoln invites Douglass to White House for advice

1865 Civil War ends; Douglass mourns assassination of Lincoln and speaks at consequent gathering in Rochester

1865 Stands for new cause to endorse black suffrage

1870 Steps up as editor-in-chief of *New National Era*

1871 President Grant appoints Douglass Commissioner to Santo Domingo, first of various presidential appointments

Commissioner to Santo Domingo

Charles Douglass

1874 Accepts position as president of Freedmen's Bank

1876 Speaks at memorial ceremony for Abraham Lincoln

1877 President Hayes appoints Douglass US marshal for the District of Columbia

1877 Meets with former master, Thomas Auld

1878 Purchases new home at Cedar Hill, near Washington, DC

1882 Wife Anna dies

1884 Marries Helen Pitts, woman's suffragist

1886 Tours Europe with Helen

1889 President Harrison appoints Douglass minister and consul to Haiti

1893 Publishes pamphlet with Ida B. Wells against racism that is distributed during World's Columbian Exposition at Chicago

1895 Dies in home at Cedar Hill on February 20, 1895

"I had a duty to perform and that was to labor and suffer with the oppressed in my native land."

Frederick Douglass

KEEP THE JOBS IN NEW BEDFORD

1

"FOUR SCORE AND SEVEN YEARS AGO . . ."

A Life Enslaved

Frederick Douglass was born in Tuckahoe, near Hillsborough, about 12 miles from Easton, in Talbot County, Maryland. He was born into slavery and grew up an innocent victim of its hardships. The institution of slavery separated mothers from their children, as Frederick experienced when his mother was sent to work on a plantation far from her infant son. The system of slavery kept records for purposes of inventory, profit, and loss. Records were often kept listing the names of those who were enslaved along with a list of the names of the horses on the plantation.

Frederick Douglass was born a slave, yet the journey he embarked upon took a road not traveled by many. He discovered literacy, the key he used to unlock freedom's door, and flung wide that door to step into manhood. Bursting onto a scene ripe with political tension and strife over the "slave issue," Douglass raised his newfound voice and challenged America.

Frederick Douglass mural in New Bedford, Massachusetts.
Photo by author

Frederick Augustus Washington Bailey was the name given to him by his mother Harriet, whose shadow was a dim comfort to him during his earliest years. Not long after Frederick was born, she was sent to work on a farm 12 miles from the cabin where he was left behind with his grandmother. Some of his earliest memories included the warmth of feeling his mother's embrace while he slept during the night. His mother walked 12 miles after a full day of hard labor to be close to her son for those few brief moments. She would then walk back those same 12 miles to return before sunrise to avoid punishment for being late to her work.

Her nighttime visits were few, given the difficulty of her situation. One day young Frederick learned that his mother had died from illness. He was about seven years old at the time.

A Log Cabin Home

The cabin where Frederick was born, took his first steps, and learned to walk was the cabin of his grandparents, Betsey and Isaac Bailey. As was common among slaveholders, small children were left with the elderly, those too old to work in the field. A number of young children, most of them probably Frederick's cousins, lived in the Bailey cabin, too.

It was a log cabin built in an impoverished district known as Tuckahoe, on the Eastern Shore of Maryland. Situated in the woods near Tuckahoe Creek, the cabin was built of clay, wood, and straw. "At a distance," Frederick said, "it resembled—though it was much smaller, less commodious and less substantial—the cabins erected in the western states by the first settlers."

Frederick loved his grandmother dearly. Her arms comforted him when he fell, and her nurturing care fashioned his earliest memories. She tenderly shielded him from the knowledge that he was a slave as long as she could.

Frederick respected his grandmother, for she was truly a remarkable woman. She was a good nurse and knew how to treat most any ailment. These were valued skills in that area, for the region of Tuckahoe, with its low marshes, swamps, and mosquitoes, was known by its residents for its fever and ague, an illness marked with fits of shaking or shivering.

The cabin where Frederick Douglass was born was probably in this grove of trees at Tappers Corner, near Tuckahoe Creek on the Eastern Shore of Maryland.
Photo by author

Betsey Bailey was an excellent fisherwoman. Her skills at net-making as well as fishing for shad and herring were known around the region. Frederick remembered seeing her stand for hours in the water up to her waist, fishing with a net using a method known as seine-hauling. For this technique, she placed the net in the water so it surrounded the fish, then drew it up by pulling a rope that was looped along its edge. The fish were gathered together as the net formed a bag around them.

Frederick's grandmother was also an expert gardener. Her methods of planting and growing sweet potatoes made her a local legend. People from neighboring areas sent for her to place their stash of seedling potatoes into the ground. During the following harvest, she was rewarded for her efforts with gifts and a share of the bountiful crop.

Frederick recalled the tender care his "Grandmother Betty" gave the seedling sweet potatoes to keep them over the winter for next year's planting. Each fall, before the cold chill of frost could damage their fragile roots, she took the seedlings inside her cabin and buried them under the floor near the fireplace.

Despite the simple memories of childhood spent under his grandmother's loving care, the shadow of slavery darkened every corner of the small rustic cabin where Frederick spent his early years. His grandmother frequently spoke with a hushed fear of "Old Master." Gradually, with an awakening of his young years, Frederick learned that his grandparents' cabin belonged to

This small cabin is reminiscent of the cabin where Frederick Douglass lived with his grandmother. Douglass had it built behind his home at Cedar Hill in Washington, DC, where it stands today.
Photo by author, courtesy National Park Service, Frederick Douglass National Historic Site

Frederick Douglass's Birthday

Unsure of the exact day, Frederick Douglass estimated the date of his birth to be in February 1817. Plantation records list his birthday in February 1818. Why did he not know the date of his birth, even though it seems records were kept? Because Frederick was born a slave. As he recalled in one of his autobiographies, "Masters allowed no questions concerning their ages to be put to them by slaves." While he was a slave, Frederick never saw the records his owners kept. When he later wrote his autobiographies, even though he tried time and time again to ask his former owners when his birthday was, he did not know what the plantation records stated.

Harriet Bailey

Frederick Douglass's mother, Harriet Bailey, was a field hand. She died while he was young. Frederick later discovered that his mother had been the only slave on the entire plantation of more than a thousand slaves who knew how to read. He cherished this knowledge as he rose from slavery to become a renowned scholar and man of letters.

"Old Master," that the woods and lot he played in belonged to "Old Master," and that even he, his grandmother, and his cousins were somehow the property of this mysterious person. Frederick later recalled, "Thus early did clouds and shadows begin to fall upon my path."

He never knew who his father was, but as a child Frederick heard whispers that it was "Old Master." His mother died before she could reveal the true identity to Frederick, but one thing was known for certain: his father was white. Once again, the institution of slavery had made its mark on Frederick. He stated realistically, "Slavery had no recognition of fathers, as none of families. That the mother was a slave was enough for its deadly purpose. By its law the child followed the condition of its mother." Brothers with the same father could be separated in life—one brother as the slave owner and the other brother as the slave. Many children born thus into the slave quarters were so fair-skinned that they looked as white as their brothers and sisters living in the master's house on the plantation. Yet they remained enslaved because the law stated that any child whose mother was a slave remained a slave as well.

Chief Clerk and Butler

Eventually, Frederick came to learn that his owner was Captain Aaron Anthony, the chief clerk and butler on an immense plantation owned by Colonel Lloyd, a plantation that was one of the most prosperous in the state of Maryland. The plantation was so large that it took over a thousand enslaved workers to maintain it. The vast property was made up of various farms with different overseers, and all these overseers answered to Captain Anthony. The captain carried the keys to Colonel Lloyd's storehouses, measured out the allowances allotted to every slave at the end of each month, oversaw all the goods brought onto the plantation, distributed the raw materials to the craftsmen, and shipped out the grain and tobacco and other produce grown on the plantation. Captain Anthony also oversaw the coopers' shop, wheelwrights' shop, blacksmiths' shop, and shoemakers' shop.

Captain Anthony had two sons and a daughter named Lucretia. His daughter had married Thomas Auld by the time Frederick was aware of the family. The captain, as he was commonly known because of his experience sailing on Chesapeake Bay, owned about 30 slaves and three farms in Tuckahoe. He lived with his family in a house on Colonel Lloyd's plantation, where he could conveniently command his post as the chief clerk and butler of the vast empire.

A Long Journey

One warm summer day, a day Frederick could never forget, his grandmother took him by the hand and led him into the woods. He could sense something was wrong, but he did not understand why deep sorrow seemed to weigh down his grandmother's shoulders like a dark cloak too heavy to bear. Mile after mile, he followed along, at times frightened by the shapes and shadows of the stumps and trees in the woods. Imagining them to be monsters eager to eat him, he clung more tightly to his grandmother's hand. At times, she toted him on her shoulders, providing a short rest for his tired legs. Finally, their long journey came to an end. Emerging from the woods, Frederick found himself surrounded by a group of children in the midst of unfamiliar buildings and houses, with men and women working in nearby fields.

Overcome with sadness, his grandmother disappeared while Frederick was being introduced to his new acquaintances, many of them his slightly older cousins. Even his brother, Perry, and sisters Sarah and Eliza were there. He had heard of them but had never met them. When Frederick turned around and discovered his grandmother was gone, he wept inconsolably, eventually sobbing himself to sleep that night. The bitter sadness that filled his heart that day haunted him for the rest of his life and became a seedbed of protest against this terrible system called slavery that held him and his loved ones in its horrible grasp.

A New Chapter in Life

Like the other children who lived in his new home at Captain Anthony's, Frederick was given only a shirt to wear. It was made of rough sackcloth and came down to his knees. The freezing days of Maryland winters were unbearable, but the nights were even worse. Frederick was always cold, and often after everyone else had gone to bed, he snuck from the kitchen closet he slept in and crawled inside a burlap sack that was used to carry corn.

Frederick Douglass walked 12 miles through these woods along Maryland's Eastern Shore when his grandmother took him from her log cabin to live at Captain Anthony's house.
Photo by author

His stomach always gnawed at him with hunger because there was never enough food to eat. Frederick remembers fighting with the dog, Old Nep, over crumbs that fell from the table where the cook prepared food for the master's family. Dipping a piece of bread into the pot of water that boiled a piece of meat was considered a luxury.

During these days of extreme hunger and harsh exposure, however, Frederick discovered a friend in Mrs. Lucretia, Captain Anthony's married daughter. Frederick learned that if he stood outside Mrs. Lucretia's window and sang a song when he was overcome with hunger, she would give him a piece of bread. This simple act of kindness toward him, as well as her occasional kindness toward others, meant a great deal.

> **"The kindness of the slavemaster only gilds the chain of slavery, and detracts nothing from its weight or power."**
> —**Frederick Douglass**

Still quite young, Frederick was not yet required to do heavy work. He was assigned small tasks such as carrying firewood, bringing in the cows, or running errands.

Yet life on a large plantation swirled around Frederick. Overseers drove the field workers. House slaves served Captain Anthony. Men, women, and children worked to supply the needs of the plantation in never-ending ways.

The things young Frederick saw and heard filled his heart with sorrow and fear. Every day, he watched other slaves be whipped or treated with brutality and cruelty. He witnessed what happened to the older children and adults who were enslaved. He knew that one day he would grow to be as old as the other slaves. Deep inside, he knew that his time of reckoning would come, and it filled him with dread.

Colonel Lloyd's Plantation

Frederick lived in Captain Anthony's house, which was situated at one end of a large green, or field. Commanding the view of the green was the colonel's stately mansion, known to everyone on the plantation as the "Great House." This was where Colonel Lloyd, Captain Anthony's employer, lived with his family, and it was a place of wealth and prominence. The Great House was the hub of the bustling and prosperous plantation.

Frederick recalled, "The road, or lane, from the gate to the great house, was richly paved with white pebbles from the beach, and, in its course, formed a complete circle around the beautiful lawn. Carriages going in and retiring from the great house made the circuit of the lawn, and their passengers were permitted to behold a scene of almost Eden-like beauty."

The Great House was a large wooden mansion, painted white, with stately columns and wings built on its sides. It was surrounded by a number of buildings, each bustling with activity. "There were kitchens," Frederick remembered, "wash-houses, dairies, summer-house, greenhouses, hen-houses, turkey-houses, pigeon-houses, and arbors, of many sizes and devices, all neatly painted, and altogether interspersed with grand old trees, ornamental and primitive, which afforded delightful shade in summer, and imparted to the scene a high degree of stately beauty."

Colonel Lloyd was a man of immense riches. All the bounties of local game, fish, and oysters from the Chesapeake Bay; vegetables and fruits from carefully tended gardens; and delicacies transported from overseas filled his tables. His family dressed in the finest fashions of the day and entertained dignitaries as well as other wealthy families. The Lloyd plantation was held in high esteem.

Leaving the Plantation Behind

When Frederick was about seven years old, his life on Colonel Lloyd's plantation suddenly came to an end. He was told that his old master, Captain Anthony, had decided to send Frederick to Baltimore, Maryland. He would live with Hugh Auld, the brother of Mrs. Lucretia's husband.

Frederick's young heart filled with joy. The next three days were remembered as some of

The lane leading up to the Great House.
Photo by author

The Great House, known as "Wye House," where Colonel Lloyd and his family lived.
Photo by author

the happiest of his life. He had heard stories of Baltimore and the fine houses that people lived in. Ever since his mother had died, he had felt lost and lonely. Even though he hadn't seen her much, he still missed his mother's warm arms wrapped around him and knowing that someone loved him as her very own. Now he hoped that he would somehow find a home and the comforts of a family, even if he were only to be serving its members as their slave.

For three days young Frederick was sent down to the creek to scrub away the filth and mange, or deadened skin, that he had gotten from his crude living conditions. Mrs. Lucretia promised him his own pair of trousers if he scrubbed himself clean. This seemed like a fine prize indeed.

Saturday finally arrived and Frederick was put on board a sloop, or small boat, heading for

Model of a sloop.
Photo by author, courtesy of Frederick Douglass–Isaac Myers Maritime Park

Baltimore. Sailing down the Miles River and away from Colonel Lloyd's plantation, Frederick took one last look at the only home he had ever known. In his heart, he said what he hoped would be a final good-bye.

Walking to the bow at the front of the ship, Frederick looked toward Baltimore with dreams of a happy future filling his every breath. For the rest of the trip, he didn't look back.

A New Home in Baltimore

Early Sunday morning, the sloop arrived at Smith's Wharf in Baltimore. After unloading a flock of sheep, Frederick accompanied one of the sailors to deliver the sheep to the slaughterhouse. From there, the sailor took Frederick to his new home, the residence of Hugh and Sophia Auld.

The Auld's house was located on Alliciana Street in an area known as Fell's Point, near one of the shipyards in Baltimore. It was here that Frederick would spend the next seven years of his boyhood.

Both Hugh and Sophia were at home when young Frederick arrived. They had a young son named Thomas and introduced him to "Freddy," as they called their new house member. It would be Frederick's duty to take care of Thomas and help watch the little boy.

During the next few years in Baltimore, Frederick learned the power that knowledge offered to those who could read and write. These lessons influenced him and shaped him into the great leader he would one day become.

As Simple as A B C

It all started innocently enough. Frederick's new owner, Sophia, taught young Frederick to read the letters of the alphabet shortly after he arrived in their home. Seeing how quickly he learned, she then began to teach him how to group three or four letters together to spell words. During one of these simple spelling lessons the master of the house, Hugh Auld, walked into the room. Seeing his wife teaching a slave to read, he insisted that the lessons stop at once.

If she taught Frederick to read, Hugh explained passionately, "There would be no keeping him. It would forever unfit him to be a slave. He would at once become unmanageable, and of no value to his master." Hugh also reminded his wife that it was against the law to teach a slave to read.

In that very instant, Frederick Douglass realized the power of reading and writing. "From that moment," he recalled, "I understood the pathway from slavery to freedom." From that point in time, with a willpower and focus that characterized many of his actions throughout the rest of his life, young Frederick resolved to take determined steps down that path toward liberty.

Frederick now had a plan. Forbidden to read in the Auld home, he enlisted the poor white children in his Baltimore neighborhood as his personal tutors.

Each time Frederick was sent on an errand through the streets of Fell's Point, he was sure to carry a book and morsels of bread with him.

Buildings along a street at Fell's Point in Baltimore, Maryland. *Photo by author*

Meeting his hungry friends in hidden alleyways, Frederick quickly exchanged the bread for what he hungered for most of all: reading lessons.

As he grew older, bonds of friendship deepened between Frederick and his white companions. Some days the boys talked about slavery, Frederick's biggest concern by the time he was about 12 years old. "I would sometimes say to them, 'I wished I could be as free as they would be when they got to be men.' . . . These words used to trouble them; they would express for me the liveliest sympathy, and console me with the hope that something would occur by which I might be free."

Even though Frederick could read, he didn't yet know how to write. He got the idea to learn how to write from his frequent visits to Durgin and Bailey's shipyard. Watching the carpenters saw the wood, Frederick observed how they wrote letters on each piece to designate its eventual position on the ship they were building. Frederick soon learned to copy and write his first four letters: *L* for larboard, *S* for starboard, *F* for forward, and *A* for aft.

"After that," Frederick remembered, "when I met with any boy who I knew could write, I would tell him I could write as well as he." This was sure to bring the response, "I don't believe you. Let me see you try it," upon which Frederick would write the four letters he knew. His friend then wrote more letters of the alphabet, and Frederick eventually learned them all.

HELP A YOUNG CHILD LEARN TO READ

Materials

* Picture book
* Beginning reader book

➡ You can help give the gift of reading to a younger child. Select a short picture book. Don't worry if it's too hard for your young friend to read or if it's above his or her independent reading level. Sit together side by side so that both of you can look at the pictures in the book together. Read the picture book aloud to your friend.

Next, choose a beginning reader book that matches your younger friend's ability to read. (To help make this choice, ask your friend's parent or teacher, or a librarian.) Invite your friend to read this book aloud to you. Help your young friend pronounce the difficult words.

Division of Property

A series of deaths in Captain Anthony's family affected the lives of Frederick Douglass and all the slaves "Old Master" had owned. Over the passage of several years, Captain Anthony died, as did his adult children, including Mrs. Lucretia. The property and the ownership of the slaves fell into the hands of Thomas Auld, Mrs. Lucretia's husband. Thomas Auld remarried and moved to

St. Michaels, a town near Colonel Lloyd's plantation on Maryland's Eastern Shore.

Frederick Douglass's life became very unstable during these years. He was, after all, counted as property. He was sent for in Baltimore and brought back to the plantation for settling the will and testament of the dead. Frederick remembered, "We were all ranked together at the valuation. Men and women, old and young, married and single, were ranked with horses, sheep, and swine." It was a time of great fear and distress. Not knowing who his next master would be, and knowing he did not have a voice in the decision, weighed heavily upon him.

He was sent back to live in Baltimore but then brought back after a time to live with Thomas Auld and his new wife in St. Michaels. He was now about 16 years old.

Slave-Breaker

What he had feared as a young child had finally come to pass. Frederick Douglass had grown up. He was now old enough and big enough to be the target of the brutalities, whippings, and cruelties he had witnessed as a young boy.

His new master and mistress claimed that city life in Baltimore had spoiled Frederick and made him unfit to be a slave. Therefore, they decided that Frederick be sent to a man in the region known as a slave-breaker.

For the first time in his life, Frederick was now a field hand. The harsh work, the gnawing

The *Columbian Orator*

When Frederick Douglass was about 12 years old he was able to save 50 cents from small coins given to him as gifts or as his own spending money. He purchased a popular schoolbook of the day, the *Columbian Orator*. Eagerly, he devoured this treasury of famous speeches and powerful documents that supported liberty and civil rights. There was even one passage where a fictional slave, after escaping three times only to be captured each time, finally convinced his master so thoroughly of the evils of slavery that the slave was set free. This book influenced Douglass deeply. It caused the passionate desire for freedom to torment him daily.

Photo by author, courtesy of Frederick Douglass–Isaac Myers Maritime Park

hunger, and the exposure to extreme weather conditions were nothing, however, compared to the inhumane and violent treatment he received at the hands of the slave-breaker. Filled with despair, Frederick admitted, "Mr. Covey succeeded in breaking me. I was broken in body, soul, and spirit."

At times Frederick was able to sneak away and stand on the nearby shore of the Chesapeake Bay. Looking out over the waters, he watched the beautiful ships sail to every corner of the globe. "I have often, in the deep stillness of a summer's Sabbath," Frederick remembered, "stood all alone upon the lofty banks of that noble bay, and traced, with saddened heart and tearful eye, the countless number of sails moving off to the mighty ocean. The sight of these always affected me powerfully. My thoughts would compel utterance; and there, with no audience but the Almighty, I would pour out my soul's complaint."

Thoughts of freedom and plans for escape flooded his mind. Standing alone on the shore, buffeted by the wind filling the white sails to speed the ships on their way, he cried out, "O God, save me! God, deliver me! Let me be free!"

Years afterward, he remembered these heartfelt prayers in the hour of his greatest despair and acknowledged that a kind Providence had heard his voice and reached down to answer his pleas. Frederick Douglass soon would experience deliverance and taste the sweet joy of freedom.

But not yet.

The Turning Point

For six months, Frederick Douglass felt overwhelmed with despair. One day, however, something snapped inside him. At the end of his strength, without hope, and the victim of repeated physical abuse, he fought back. To his surprise, he was stronger than the slave-breaker —and he won the fight. After that, Mr. Covey was afraid to fight Frederick again. That battle was the turning point for him as a slave. Not only did he become known and feared by the slaveholders in the area, but he determined to flee to freedom no matter what the cost.

He was sent to live with and work for a different master. In his new home he met new friends, and with them he planned his escape.

Sabbath School

In the summer of 1835 Frederick Douglass started a secret school to teach fellow slaves to read. Meeting first behind the barn or in the woods, he eventually asked a free African American to meet in his home. In spite of great danger and peril of discovery, over 40 students from local plantations snuck away on Sundays to gather in the small cabin. Each brought a copy of *Webster's Spelling-Book*, forgotten by their masters who had outgrown that common textbook but now cherished by the slaves as a pathway to knowledge and freedom. Frederick Douglass taught them to read the Bible. Feeling a deep sense of satisfaction from helping his fellow sufferers, years later he learned that several of his pupils cast off the chains of slavery and escaped to freedom.

It started with the dawn of the new year. Frederick vowed that he would not let 1836 pass without making an honest attempt to escape the chains that chafed so heavily against his soul.

He brought his closest friends and relatives into his confidence as he organized his plan. The Easter holidays were quickly approaching. Frederick said, "The plan of escape which I recommended, and to which my comrades assented, was to take a large canoe, owned by Mr. Hamilton, and, on the Saturday night previous to the Easter holidays, launch out into the Chesapeake Bay, and paddle for its head—a distance of seventy miles—with all our might."

Preparations were made. Frederick wrote a pass for each member of his group, five in all, to show to anyone if they were questioned along their route. He signed it with the signature of William Hamilton, the master who owned two members of the group. The pass read as follows:

This is to certify, that I, the undersigned, have given the bearer, my servant, full liberty to go to Baltimore, and spend the Easter holidays. Written with mine own hand, &c., 1835.

William Hamilton,
Near St. Michael's,
in Talbot County, Maryland

The day of escape dawned. Worry had made it impossible for Frederick to sleep. The fear of being caught and killed, or sold south where he'd heard slavery was even more cruel than in Maryland—combined with a fear of unknown dangers—was very real. Frederick and his friends woke up and, under the pretence that nothing was planned, started their usual morning chores in the barn and in the fields.

And then it happened.

Site of the Talbot County jail where Frederick Douglass and friends were imprisoned after his first attempt to escape. This building was constructed in 1878 and replaced the original. *Photo by author*

Slavery

— ◆ —

by George Moses Horton

Slavery, thou peace-disturbing thief,
We can't but look with frowns on thee,
Without the balm which gives relief,
The balm of birthright—Liberty.

Thy wing has been for ages furl'd,
Thy vessel toss'd from wave to wave,
By stormy winds 'mid billows hurl'd—
Such is the fate of every slave.

A loathsome burden we are to bear,
Through sultry bogs we trudging go;
Thy rusty chains we frown to wear,
Without one inch of wealth to show.

Our fathers from their native land
Were dragged across the brackish deep,
Bound fast together, hand in hand,
O! did the God of nature sleep?

When sadly thro' the almond grove
The pirate dragged them o'er the sod,
Devoid of pity and of love,
They seemed as left without a God.

Are we not men as well as they,
Born to enjoy the good of earth,
Brought in creation from the clay,
To reap a blessing from our birth?

Alas! how can such rebels thrive,
Who take our lives and wealth away,
Since all were placed on earth to live,
And prosper by the light of day.

The maledictions* of our God,
Pervade the dwindling world we see;
He hurls the vengeance with his rod,
And thunders, let the slave be free!

Maledictions are declarations that something is terribly wrong.

Reprinted from *The Black Bard of North Carolina: George Moses Horton and his Poetry*, edited by Joan R. Sherman. Copyright © 1997 by the University of North Carolina Press. Used by permission of the publisher. www.uncpress.unc.edu

Men galloped up on horseback. The sheriff and constables hurried to the scene, armed with pistols and clubs. The conspirators were arrested. They had been betrayed! Someone had told their secret.

Frederick and his four friends were tied with ropes and dragged behind horses for a 15-mile walk to the Talbot County jail in Easton.

> **"Does a righteous God govern the universe? and for what does he hold the thunders in his right hand, if not to smite the oppressor, and deliver the spoiled out of the hand of the spoiler?"**
> —Frederick Douglass

A New Direction

Someone had betrayed their secret, but Frederick and his friends were determined not to betray each other. Just before his arrest, Frederick tossed his pass into the fireplace. His urgent whispers to his friends during the long walk to jail convinced them to eat the passes they still carried in their pockets.

Though they were questioned many times when they reached the Talbot County jail, Frederick and his friends did not reveal their plans. To do so could have meant their death.

Without any proof, Frederick's friends were returned to their masters. Thomas Auld, Frederick's owner, decided to send Frederick back to Baltimore after his three years away, to live again as the slave of his brother, Hugh Auld. This decision was based on threats from local slaveholders to kill Frederick if he remained on the Eastern Shore of Maryland because he was now known as the leader of an attempted escape.

In Baltimore, plans were made for Frederick to learn the trade of caulking a boat. Caulking was a method where workers pounded strands of cotton fibers in between the wooden planks of a ship to make it watertight. Baltimore was a busy port with wharfs, docks, and shipyards. Hugh Auld sent Frederick to learn the trade of caulking in one of the nearby shipyards.

At that time, however, there was a great conflict in Baltimore. The whites feared their jobs would be lost to free blacks or slaves who were forced to work for lower wages or no wages at all. At one point the whites in the shipyard where Frederick was apprenticed threatened to strike. They said they would not work at all unless only whites were hired in the shipyard. To make matters even worse, a group of these laborers attacked Frederick. Unable to hold his ground against the gang of four large, burly men, he was seriously injured.

During the time Frederick stayed at home allowing his wounds to heal, Hugh Auld decided to take him to a different shipyard. Several years earlier, Hugh had owned his own shipyard, but

(left) Quilt: "Pullin' Oakum," by Joanne Harris, 2006.
Photo by author, courtesy of Frederick Douglass–Isaac Myers Maritime Park

(below) Frederick Douglass was apprenticed in a Baltimore shipyard to learn the trade of caulking. Note his name listed here as Fred Bailey. Bailey was his given name, but he changed his name to Douglass after escaping to freedom in order to avoid capture by slave hunters.
Photo by author, courtesy of Frederick Douglass–Isaac Myers Maritime Park

Caulking a Boat

To caulk a boat, workers used a special wooden caulking mallet, or type of hammer, to pound strings of fibers between the boat's wooden planks. For smaller boats, strands of cotton fibers were used. For the large seafaring ships found in many Baltimore shipyards, thicker strands of oakum were used. Oakum was made from hemp fibers, or special plant fibers, that had been soaked in pitch or tar. Caulkers such as Frederick Douglass positioned a strand of oakum into the seam, or crack, between two wooden planks of a ship and held it in position with a caulking iron, or type of chisel. They pounded on the iron with the caulking mallet, driving the oakum into the crack.

Caulking tools from left to right: caulking mallet, caulking iron, and oakum. *Photo by author, courtesy of Frederick Douglass–Isaac Myers Maritime Park*

due to hard financial times he had to let it go. Now he was foreman at Walter Price's shipyard. Hugh took Frederick to Price's shipyard, which was where Frederick finally learned his trade.

Frederick was a quick learner. In no time at all, he learned how to use his caulking tools with skill. Within a year he had moved from apprentice caulker, or one who was learning how to caulk, to the position of expert caulker. Frederick remembers, "In the course of a single year, I was able to command the highest wages paid to journeymen caulkers in Baltimore."

Frederick earned about $1.50 per day at his job. Some weeks, during the busy season, he was able to earn up to $9.00 a week, quite an impressive salary in the late 1830s for his line of work! But since he was a slave, these wages were not his own. Instead, the money was handed over to his master, Hugh Auld.

The Ties That Bind

For the first time in his life, Frederick developed deep friendships with free blacks, a number of them his own age. "Many of the young calkers," he recalled, "could read, write, and cipher. Some of them had high notions about mental improvement; and the free ones, on Fell's Point, organized what they called the 'East Baltimore Mental Improvement Society.'"

His new friends welcomed Frederick into their society. The debates they held stirred Frederick's heart. Recognizing his natural gift for speaking, they assigned Frederick a leading position in several of their debates. Little did he realize that his experiences in this group would help prepare him for his greatest achievements as a famous orator.

But not yet. Frederick was still a slave, even while many of his new friends were free. As Frederick became more skilled in his trade, his discontent grew. Why should he be required to turn over all his wages to another man? Why shouldn't he be able to keep his wages as his friends did? He was more determined than ever before to plan his escape.

As he considered all the different avenues for escaping slavery, Frederick realized he could buy his way to freedom. Some people purchased their freedom outright from their masters. Others escaped by purchasing false identity papers, train tickets, and costumes to disguise themselves.

Frederick asked his owner for permission to "hire his own time," or find his own employment. This was common practice in that era. A slave who hired his own time was able to save up money for himself if he worked long, hard hours. After being refused permission from Thomas Auld (his actual owner), Frederick requested permission from Hugh Auld, his master in Baltimore.

Hugh gave Frederick permission to hire his own time under strict conditions: he would have to find his own jobs, collect his own pay, provide his own clothes, find his own place to live, and buy his own caulking tools. And every Saturday, Frederick had to pay Hugh three dollars.

FORM A DEBATE CLUB

➡ One of Frederick Douglass's earliest exposures to public speaking came when he joined a debate club in Baltimore. You can form a debate club with your friends, too.

To start, look for a place where your club can meet and determine how often you want to meet. Gather reference materials to prepare for the debates, such as dictionaries, encyclopedias, newspapers, magazines, and a computer with access to the Internet.

Plan to meet to prepare for the debates, practice mock debates, and hold actual debates. Appoint leaders of the club, such as president, secretary, and treasurer. Invite parents, teachers, or older friends to be coaches or judges.

Choose which debate format your group will use, and learn its procedures. The Lincoln-Douglas Debate, or LD Debate, is one of the most common formats debate clubs use today. This format is based on the type of debates Abraham Lincoln and Stephen Douglas used to argue their stand on the issue of slavery in the 1850s. It is a values-based debate where members focus on an issue of philosophical or political concern. You can learn more about LD Debate in *The Ultimate Lincoln-Douglas Debate Handbook* by Marko Djuranovic, or explore different debate formats by visiting the International Debate Education Association website at www.idebate.org/teaching/debate_formats.php.

Anna Murray worked as a domestic, or house servant, in Baltimore.
Photo by author, courtesy of Frederick Douglass–Isaac Myers Maritime Park

"This was a hard bargain," Frederick remembered. "The wear and tear of clothing, the losing and breaking of tools, and the expense of board, made it necessary for me to earn at least six dollars per week, to keep even with the world." Yet it was a bargain Frederick was willing to take.

A New Friend

Now that Frederick had permission to hire his own time, his hours were his own. Among the deep friendships he formed in Baltimore, he found a new friend when he met Anna Murray.

Anna was part of the small circle of young, free blacks in Baltimore who welcomed into their group this hardworking and discontented visionary named Frederick Bailey. The young couple fell in love. With Anna, Frederick now shared his deepest desires for freedom. He found a sympathetic listener. Anna was determined to do whatever she could to help Frederick escape.

That year, 1838, from May to August, Frederick worked hard and saved every penny he could. Every Saturday night that summer, he returned to his master and handed over the money according to their agreement.

One Saturday, however, he was kept working in the shipyard later than usual.

Frederick had made plans with his friends to attend a local camp meeting that Saturday night. The camp meeting was about 12 miles from Baltimore. Finally finished at the shipyard, Frederick knew it was getting late. He simply wouldn't have time to go back to his master's house and then head off to the camp meeting.

Frederick made a decision that would change his life. He decided to go to the camp meeting and pay the money to his master when he returned.

At camp meetings such as this one, Frederick found a faith he could believe in. Having grown up with slaveholders who belonged to the local churches, he had been told twisted lies that God created black men to be slaves. At the camp meetings, however, the preachers spoke about a loving God who valued each individual and created all people as equals. Hearing this message, Frederick embraced Christianity as his faith.

He stayed at the camp meeting one day longer than he had planned. When it was over, however, he headed straight to the house of his master, Hugh Auld, to pay the money they had agreed upon.

He found a furious man waiting for him. Thinking that Frederick had escaped, Hugh punished him. Hugh took away Frederick's right to hire his own time and therefore crushed his escape plans.

This was a devastating blow. Frederick could no longer take this kind of unfair treatment. He was determined to take action. He must escape! Now, before it was too late!

2

"OUR FATHERS BROUGHT FORTH ON THIS CONTINENT . . ."

Stepping into Freedom

Frederick Augustus Washington Bailey knew he must escape now—or perhaps never. Even though he was still enslaved, he had tasted what it was like to move freely through the streets of Baltimore, find his own jobs, and choose his own activities throughout the day. Now those privileges were denied him. All too well, he understood how his life could change in one moment due to the wishes of his master. He couldn't risk being sent back to working on a plantation on the Eastern Shore of Maryland or, even worse, being sold farther south. He must escape now.

Frederick picked a date: September 3, 1838. Just three weeks away! He whispered his plans to Anna. He would flee to New York City and then send for her when he was standing safely on the soil of a free state. She would follow, and they would be married. Neither of them dared to think of what might happen if their plans did not work.

The wedding of Frederick Douglass and Anna Murray.
Photo by author, courtesy of Frederick Douglass–Isaac Myers Maritime Park

The next three weeks were spent in frenzied preparation. Anna helped fashion Frederick a sailor's outfit, putting her sewing skills to good use. From her earnings, she helped pay for Frederick's journey as well as her own. There were tickets to be purchased for passage on carriages, trains, and steamships. She packed everything she owned to be ready for his call to join him at his side. A featherbed with pillows, sheets and blankets for the bed, dishes and knives and forks and spoons—she planned to take as much as she could for the new life ahead of them.

Anna even packed one trunk with a new silk dress. Carefully folding the beautiful, soft, plum-colored fabric to fit inside the trunk, she hoped that she would soon wear the dress on their wedding day. For now, though, she tried to keep her hands busy so that worry would not overwhelm her.

A Household Servant

For most of the previous decade, Anna had lived in Baltimore working as a domestic, or maid. She had lived with her parents in Denton, Caroline County, Maryland, until she was 17 years old. She then moved to Baltimore where she found work living with the Montells, a French family who needed a household servant. After working with them for two years, Anna found employment serving the Wells family, who also lived in Baltimore. Mr. Wells was postmaster at that time.

During those years, Anna worked hard to serve the members of the Wells household. A special bond grew between her and her employers, and afterward she always spoke with fondness of the years spent with the family.

Anna Murray packed her belongings in trunks such as these as she prepared to join Frederick in New York City after his escape.
Photo by author, courtesy of Frederick Douglass–Isaac Myers Maritime Park

Slave? Or Free?

Bambarra Murray and his wife, Mary, were slaves. Together, they had seven children. According to the law that children were slaves if their mother was a slave, each of the couple's children was born into slavery. However, in 1813, both Bambarra and Mary acquired their freedom. Just one month after being set free, they had their eighth child. They named their new precious little girl Anna. Oh, what joy must have filled their hearts as they held their little baby close in their arms! Because Anna had been born *after* her mother was listed on the court records as free, little Anna was born into freedom. Her parents had four more children, all born into freedom too.

Industrious, independent, and dependable, Anna was responsible for many of the day-to-day household duties in the home of the Wellses. Cooking the meals, polishing the silver, and washing the laundry were probably some of the tasks she tended to.

Freedom's Flight

For nine years, Anna Murray had worked as a maid for families living in Baltimore. Now, however, her future was uncertain. As she helped Frederick prepare for his escape, she knew she must leave all her friends and connections behind. The three weeks of preparation were filled with anxiety.

At that time, the state of Maryland required free African Americans to carry "free papers" at all times. Frederick explained, "In these papers the name, age, color, height, and form of the free man were described, together with any scars or other marks upon his person which could assist in his identification." Sailors carried "sailor's protection papers," similar to these free papers, to provide proof of their free status as well.

It was a secret practice among fugitives to borrow or pay someone to use their free papers and then mail them back to their owner once the fugitive had arrived in a free state. Although Frederick had a number of friends who were free and carried free papers, he did not match the description on any of his friends' papers.

One of Frederick's friends was a sailor who was free. He agreed to let Frederick use his

"TO TAKE OFF SPOTS OF ANY SORT, FROM ANY KIND OF CLOTH"

Anna Murray probably made her own soap to scrub the laundry, such as the soap found in this recipe from The House Servant's Directory *by Robert Roberts.*

Materials

* ⅔ cup honey
* 1 egg yolk
* 1 tablespoon table salt
* Wooden spoon
* Mixing bowl
* Pair of old, dirty socks you can throw away
* Old-fashioned washboard, or 1 x 2-foot plain pine board
* Large bucket or laundry tub

➡ Mix the honey, egg yolk, and salt together in the bowl. Working on a protected surface, use the wooden spoon to spread a thick paste on your dirty socks. Allow the mixture to soak into the socks for at least an hour, or overnight. Place the washboard in a large bucket or laundry tub that is half full of

warm water. Scrub the socks up and down on the washboard to try to remove the dirt. Rinse the socks well. Hang them in the sun to dry.

As a maid, Anna Murray used a washboard like this to scrub the laundry for the Wells family. Photo by author, courtesy of Frederick Douglass–Isaac Myers Maritime Park

Robert Roberts (c. 1777–1860)

Robert Roberts served elite families in Boston. When he was hired to serve as a butler to the governor and later senator of Massachusetts Christopher Gore, Roberts drew from his years of exemplary service to write a book of recipes and instructions for being a top-rate servant.

Roberts published his book, *The House Servant's Directory,* in 1827. It was one of the first books published by an African American. Even if Anna Murray did not ever read *The House Servant's Directory* herself, this book gives us a glimpse into the duties and tasks she would have been responsible for as a maid serving a family in America during the 1830s.

The House Servant's Directory by Robert Roberts. Courtesy Special Collections, Michigan State University Libraries

THE
HOUSE SERVANT'S DIRECTORY,
OR
A MONITOR FOR PRIVATE FAMILIES :
COMPRISING
HINTS ON THE ARRANGEMENT AND PERFORMANCE OF
SERVANTS' WORK,
WITH GENERAL RULES FOR
SETTING OUT TABLES AND SIDEBOARDS
IN FIRST ORDER ;
THE ART OF WAITING
IN ALL ITS BRANCHES ; AND LIKEWISE HOW TO CONDUCT
LARGE AND SMALL PARTIES
WITH ORDER ;
WITH GENERAL DIRECTIONS FOR PLACING ON TABLE
ALL KINDS OF JOINTS, FISH, FOWL, &c.
WITH
FULL INSTRUCTIONS FOR CLEANING
PLATE, BRASS, STEEL, GLASS, MAHOGANY ;
AND LIKEWISE
ALL KINDS OF PATENT AND COMMON LAMPS :
OBSERVATIONS
ON SERVANTS' BEHAVIOUR TO THEIR EMPLOYERS ;
AND UPWARDS OF
100 VARIOUS AND USEFUL RECEIPTS,
CHIEFLY COMPILED
FOR THE USE OF HOUSE SERVANTS ;
AND IDENTICALLY MADE
TO SUIT THE MANNERS AND CUSTOMS OF FAMILIES
IN THE UNITED STATES.

By ROBERT ROBERTS.
WITH
FRIENDLY ADVICE TO COOKS
AND HEADS OF FAMILIES,
AND COMPLETE DIRECTIONS HOW TO BURN
LEHIGH COAL.

BOSTON,
MUNROE AND FRANCIS, 128 WASHINGTON-STREET.
NEW YORK,
CHARLES S. FRANCIS, 189 BROADWAY.
1827.

---

sailor's protection papers to escape. Frederick knew this was a serious danger. If someone asked to read his papers, that person would realize instantly that the papers were not Frederick's because Frederick did not match the description. He would be arrested immediately. The consequences would be terrible.

Frederick carefully planned his escape. He decided to travel openly from Baltimore to Philadelphia and then to New York City. Dressed as a sailor, he planned to carry his friend's sailor's protection papers in his pocket. He would pretend he was free and travel like free people did—on the train, on the ferry, and on the steamboat. It was a risk, but one he hoped would work.

Part of his escape plan, therefore, was to do everything he could to avoid having anyone actually read the papers he carried. He made arrangements for another friend to arrive at the train station in Baltimore with Frederick's luggage at the exact moment the train was starting to leave.

Timing everything down to the second, his luggage arrived as planned, and Frederick jumped up on the steps of the train just as it started to leave the station. It looked like Frederick did not have time to stand in line and purchase his ticket at the train station where the ticket master would have demanded his papers and instantly spotted his deceit.

Frederick was impersonating a sailor. He remembered, "I had on a red shirt and a tarpaulin hat and black cravat, tied in sailor fashion, carelessly and loosely about my neck. My knowledge of ships and sailors' talk came much to my assistance, for I knew a ship from stem to stern, and from keelson to crosstrees, and could talk sailor like an 'old salt.'" His friend's sailor's protection papers were hidden deep inside his pocket.

As Frederick had hoped, the train conductor was busy collecting tickets. By the time he reached Frederick, the conductor asked, "I suppose you have your free papers?"

It was the most anxious moment Frederick ever experienced in his life. Trying to hide his fear, Frederick answered quickly, "No, sir; I never carry my free papers to sea with me."

"But you have something to show that you are a free man, have you not?" the conductor asked.

"Yes, sir," Frederick answered, his heart pounding. "I have a paper with the American eagle on it, that will carry me round the world."

He reached in his pocket and pulled out the borrowed papers, boasting the large image of the American eagle that was on every sailor's protection papers. Without taking the time to read it, the conductor collected Frederick's money for his ticket and moved on to other passengers.

Frederick let out a deep sigh of relief. He closed his eyes and steadied himself.

The first main obstacle had passed.

He was on a train, speeding north, clutching a ticket in his hand.

MAKE A PASTE TO KEEP FLIES AWAY

The House Servant's Directory by Robert Roberts was a very practical book. It even included a recipe for making a mixture that was guaranteed to chase away the flies, a pesky problem in the mid-1800s.

Materials

* ½ teaspoon ground black pepper
* 1 teaspoon brown sugar
* 1 tablespoon fresh cream (heavy cream or whipping cream from fresh milk found in the supermarket dairy section, not a processed can of dessert topping)
* Whisk
* Small bowl
* Spoon
* Plate

➡ Mix the pepper, brown sugar, and cream together in a small bowl using a whisk. Spoon the mixture onto a plate. Place the plate in a room where flies are a bother and see if they disappear! Be sure to keep the mixture away from pets or small children.

DRESS LIKE A SAILOR

When Frederick Douglass escaped, he disguised himself as a sailor. A sailor in the mid-1830s wore a red shirt, a tarpaulin hat, and a black cravat tied loosely around his neck. Most sailors made their own tarpaulin hats by stitching fabric from old sails into the shape of a hat and then painting the hat with tar. This made the hat waterproof, which helped protect a sailor from the splashing waves and pelting rain from storms at sea.

Tarpaulin Hat Materials

* String
* Ruler
* Pencil
* Scissors
* 1 yard white cotton duck fabric
* White thread
* Sewing needle
* Thimble
* Pins
* Newspapers
* 4 ounces black glossy acrylic fabric paint
* Wax paper
* Clear tape
* Paper plate
* Paintbrush

Adult supervision required

➡ Measure your head by wrapping the string around your head over your forehead where you would wear a hat. Next, measure this length of string with your ruler. The instructions for making this hat will fit your head if it is 23 or 24 inches around. Adjust the patterns slightly if your head is smaller or larger.

Tie a piece of string to a pencil and cut the string to be 6½ inches from the pencil to the end of the string. Mark a dot 7 inches away from all edges of the cotton duck fabric. Hold the end of the string on the dot with one hand. With your other hand, hold the pencil and draw a 13-inch circle, with the dot as the middle of the circle.

Draw another circle the same way, only this time cut the string to measure 4¼ inches. The finished circle will measure 8½ inches across.

Cut out the two circles from the cotton duck fabric.

Inside the 13-inch circle, draw a smaller circle. Cut the string to measure 4 inches. Hold the end of the string on the dot in the center. With your other hand, hold the pencil and draw an 8-inch circle. Cut out the smaller circle and discard it.

Use your ruler to measure a 3 x 24-inch rectangle and cut this strip out of the cotton duck fabric.

Fold the rectangle in half and use the needle and thread to stitch the two short edges together with small stitches as close together as possible. Wear the thimble to protect your finger while you sew because it can be hard to push the needle through the cotton duck fabric.

Pin one long edge of the strip to the small circle and stitch the edges together with small stitches as close together as possible.

Pin the other long edge of the strip to the inside edge of the large circle as shown. Stitch the edges together with many small stitches as close together as possible.

Spread out sheets of newspaper to cover a table, for protection. Tape two sheets of wax paper together to form a large square big enough for the hat to sit on. Place the hat on the wax paper on top of the newspaper. Pour a puddle of fabric paint on a paper plate and use the paintbrush to paint the entire top side of the hat. Allow the paint to dry completely overnight, gently repositioning the hat several times to prevent it from sticking to the wax paper while it dries. Weigh down the brim of the hat with a small object if it starts to curl up during the drying process.

After the hat is completely dry, turn it over. Use a new square of wax paper for it to sit on. Carefully paint just the underside of the hat's brim, stopping short of the stitches. Do not paint the stitches or the inside of the hat because then it will be uncomfortable to wear. If the brim starts to sag while you are painting it, crumble squares of wax paper into balls and prop up the brim of the hat with them until it dries. Allow the hat to finish drying overnight.

Cravat Materials

* ½ yard lightweight black cotton fabric
* Scissors
* Sewing needle
* Black thread
* Ruler

➥ Cut the piece of fabric in half lengthwise to form two long, thin 9-inch strips. Sew these strips end to end to form one long, thin strip of fabric. Use the ruler to measure, and cut the strip to be 64 inches long.

Lay the strip flat on a table. Grasp the fabric strip in the middle and loosely roll the middle section into a tube. Place this behind your neck and over your shoulders like a scarf, allowing the ends to hang down the front.

Adjust the fabric so that the right end hangs about 3 inches longer than the other. Cross the long end over the short end to form a *V* about 4 inches below your neck. The long end will now point to the left. Draw the long end behind the short end, up inside the loop, and over and down to the left side again.

Cross the long end over the short end again. The long end will now be pointing to the right. Bring the long end behind the short end, up through the small loop, and out again to the right.

Tighten the knot and adjust the cravat to hang loosely around your neck.

A Dangerous Day

Over the next 24 hours, peril and danger awaited Frederick at every turn of his journey. "The heart of no fox or deer," he recalled, "with hungry hounds on his trail, in full chase, could have beaten more anxiously or noisily than did mine from the time I left Baltimore till I reached Philadelphia."

At Havre de Grace, Maryland, the train stopped. Frederick joined other passengers traveling across the Susquehanna River and boarded a ferry. One of the workers on the ferry recognized Frederick and started to ask him questions. Alarmed, Frederick hurried to the other side of the boat.

Once on shore at the other side of the river, Frederick boarded another train and spotted even more people he knew! One was an overseer he'd recently worked for at a shipyard and another was a German blacksmith he knew well. At any moment any one of them could have ruined his chance to escape. But none did.

Finally, he reached the most dangerous part of his journey. "The last point of imminent danger," Frederick shared, "and the one I dreaded most, was Wilmington." In Wilmington, Delaware, he left the train and boarded a steamboat. Frederick knew that the borders between slave states and free states were the most perilous of all. Slave hunters flocked to Wilmington to look for men and women escaping to freedom. Would they be searching for his face today among the crowd?

Officials in border towns such as Wilmington were extra cautious and carefully inspected every African American crossing over the state line into the free states. Would they stop him now and demand to read his papers?

Frederick remembered, "In making the change I again apprehended arrest, but no one disturbed me, and I was soon on the broad and beautiful Delaware [River], speeding away to the Quaker City."

The Final Stretch on Freedom's Road

Frederick stepped off the steamboat and onto the dock at Philadelphia, Pennsylvania, as a free man. Yet he knew his freedom was still not secure. He was too near the slave catchers. Too close to the slave states.

As the afternoon sun shone upon his back that warm September day, Frederick knew his journey was not yet over. He would not jeopardize his newfound freedom by staying so close to those who could easily capture him and return him to slavery. He walked slowly along the docks, smelling the familiar smells of fish and boats and the river, not quite sure where to go next.

Stopping a fellow African American, Frederick asked how he could travel to New York City. The man directed him to the train depot, located on Willow Street.

As Frederick walked through Philadelphia on the way to the Willow Street depot, the setting sun cast his lengthening shadow along the cobblestone streets. The evening air turned cooler. Glimpses of Independence Hall could be seen through the trees.

What thoughts stirred his heart, knowing that now each step he took was the step of a free man? Did he know that others had come before him, walking through these streets with thoughts of freedom burning in their souls? Founding Fathers Thomas Jefferson, Benjamin Franklin, and John Adams had walked these same streets over 50 years earlier when meeting to declare their independence from British rule. In the years following the American Revolution, Black Founders Richard Allen, Absalom Jones, and James Forten walked these same streets leading Philadelphia's community of free blacks in the campaign for equal rights through the sermons they preached, the petitions they signed, and the newspaper articles they wrote.

A new generation of freedom fighters was living and working in this city now, black and white together, determined to bring the evils of slavery to an end. Little could Frederick imagine that he would one day join them. Little could he dream that his voice would one day echo through these streets alongside theirs, rallying the cry for freedom.

His one consuming thought was to travel as quickly toward his destination as possible. His flight to freedom was not yet over. Even though

he was walking on free soil, he was still in too much danger.

He found the Willow Street train depot, boarded a train, and went speeding through the night on his way to New York City.

Morning dawned. The train whistle blew as it chugged to a stop. Blasts of steam filled the air. Frederick stepped out into the crisp, fall morning of a bustling metropolis. His 24-hour flight had come to an end.

He was free—he had broken the chains of slavery! He had thrown off the terrible and powerful bonds that had chafed against him all his life.

The Willow Street train depot in Philadelphia was located in full view of Independence Hall. It was here Frederick Douglass purchased a train ticket to New York City on September 3, 1838, the day he escaped from slavery. This short segment of tracks shows where the Willow Street train depot once operated.
Photo by author

> "From my earliest recollections of serious matters, I date the entertainment of something like an ineffaceable conviction, that slavery would not always be able to hold me within its foul embrace; and this conviction, like a word of living faith, strengthened me through the darkest trials of my lot. This good spirit was from God; and to him I offer thanksgiving and praise."
>
> —Frederick Douglass

Alone and in Despair

Frederick walked the streets of New York City. "It was a moment of the highest excitement I ever experienced," he remembered. Heart bursting with joy and relief, he said, "I felt like one who had escaped a den of hungry lions."

This feeling quickly disappeared, however, in the distress of knowing he was still in danger. A fugitive, he could always be captured and sent back into slavery. Frederick was overcome by a deep sense of loneliness. Who could he trust? A price was now on his head and anyone who turned him in, black or white, could profit. He looked at all the people around him. He said, "I dared not to unfold to any one of them my sad condition. I was afraid to speak to any one for fear of speaking to the wrong one."

Unexpectedly, he met one person he knew well while wandering through the city's streets, a fugitive like himself. His friend confirmed his fears. "Trust no one!" his friend warned before disappearing back into the sea of people. Confused, lonely, and afraid, Frederick wandered the streets of New York City for several days. At night, he slept in alleys or at the docks. Finally, close to despair, he found a sailor who seemed to have an honest face.

"I told him I was running for my freedom—knew not where to go—money almost gone—was hungry—thought it unsafe to go the shipyards for work, and needed a friend." Frederick had found a friend at last. The sailor made arrangements for the lonely fugitive to meet David Ruggles.

A Helping Hand

New York City had a core group of men and women who helped the countless fugitives pouring into their city who were penniless, scared of capture, and close to starving. David Ruggles was one of their leaders. A dedicated abolitionist, Ruggles was the secretary of the New York Vigilance Committee, a group that kept watch for escaping slaves to help them reach safety along the Underground Railroad.

Frederick remembered, "Mr. Ruggles was the first officer on the underground railroad with whom I met after reaching the north, and indeed, the first of whom I ever heard anything." Gradually, Frederick learned all about the Underground Railroad. He learned that men and women who helped fugitive slaves were called officers and conductors. Officers and conductors provided food, warm clothing, and a place to sleep to the fugitives. They hid fugitives in secret hideouts until arrangements could be made to send them safely on their way. Some officers and conductors on the Underground Railroad bought tickets for passage on trains, boats, or carriages for fugitives who showed up at their doors. Others transported these men, women, and children by

Abolitionist David Ruggles hid Frederick for several days in a house that stood on this site at 36 Lispenard Street.
Photo by author

THE CURRENT WORLD SLAVE MARKET

Adult supervision recommended

➡ The global economic crisis has affected the existence of slavery in the world today. Poor people in many countries are still forced to work against their will.

Organizations such as UNICEF and World Vision work hard to help people who are forced to live or work in slave-like conditions. The United Nations endorses rights that every child should have.

Explore opportunities to help at organizations such as UNICEF (www.unicef.org) or World Vision (www.WorldVision.org) or even at a local church or trusted community organization. You can make donations, sponsor a child, organize a fund-raiser, help provide assistance after a natural disaster, or join discussions on important worldwide issues.

David Ruggles (1810-1849)

Famous in antislavery circles, David Ruggles, along with his fellow abolitionists in New York City, helped over 1,000 fugitives on their journey to freedom. When a poor, hungry, unknown fugitive arrived in the city, Ruggles helped him too. Little did Ruggles know this man he helped would become the most famous abolitionist of all, Frederick Douglass!

Courtesy of the Library of Congress, LC-USZ62-90789

Plaque of the marriage certificate.
Photo by author, courtesy of Frederick Douglass–Isaac Myers Maritime Park

Frederick Johnson–Anna Murray Marriage Certificate

"This may certify, that I joined together in holy matrimony Frederick Johnson and Anna Murray, as man and wife, in the presence of Mr. David Ruggles and Mrs. Michaels.

James W. C. Pennington.
New York, Sept. 15, 1838."

hiding them in wagons or leading them on foot by night to the next stop. Each stop at the Underground Railroad had secret hideouts where the fugitives hid until arrangements could be made to send them safely to the next stop.

Ruggles took Frederick to 36 Lispenard Street, where he had a bookstore and reading room. There, he hid Frederick for several days until Anna Murray could arrive to meet him.

> "God and right stood vindicated. I WAS A FREEMAN, and the voice of peace and joy thrilled my heart."
> —Frederick Douglass

The Dawn of Happiness

Frederick sent word to Anna Murray that he had reached New York City. Quickly, she finished packing her trunks. She hurried from Baltimore to 36 Lispenard Street, where Frederick was hiding from kidnappers, safe in the hands of the New York Vigilance Committee. A group of abolitionists, the New York Vigilance Committee was one of the most influential and active forces against slavery in America, helping over 1,000 fugitives on their flight to freedom.

Arrangements were made for Frederick and Anna's marriage. Reverend James W. C. Pennington performed the ceremony while Ruggles and another friend looked on. Frederick Bailey was advised to choose a new last name to use in order to avoid being discovered by kidnappers, and he chose the name of Johnson. Pennington pronounced the new Mr. and Mrs. Johnson as man and wife. It was a happy day.

When Ruggles learned that Frederick was a caulker, he recommended the newlyweds move to New Bedford, Massachusetts. Ruggles was certain Frederick could find work there. He also knew there was an active branch of the Underground Railroad operating in New Bedford under the capable hands of Nathan Johnson and his wife, Mary (called Polly). Ruggles sent the young couple on their way.

Frederick and Anna left New York City on a steamer bound for Newport, Rhode Island. They then traveled the final leg of their journey by stagecoach. "Thus," Frederick recalled, "in one fortnight after my flight from Maryland, I was safe in New Bedford, regularly entered upon the exercise of the rights, responsibilities, and duties of a freeman."

A New Home

Frederick and Anna Johnson arrived at the home of Nathan and Mary Johnson in New Bedford. The young couple was overwhelmed by the generosity of these kind abolitionists. Learning that their trunks had been kept by the stagecoach driver until Frederick could pay for his fare, Nathan Johnson immediately loaned Frederick the two dollars he needed to retrieve his baggage.

The newly married couple disembarked from a steamer at the wharf in Newport, Rhode Island, and took a stagecoach to New Bedford, Massachusetts.
Courtesy of Documenting the American South, the University of North Carolina at Chapel Hill Libraries

Once the trunks were secure, the Johnsons offered a home to Frederick and Anna. They unpacked their few possessions, and Anna set up housekeeping.

The question of Frederick's new name came up. Nathan Johnson recommended he choose a different name. There were already too many Johnsons living in New Bedford. Mentioning that he was reading *The Lady of the Lake*, a poem

James William Charles Pennington (c. 1807–1870)

Reverend James W. C. Pennington was still a fugitive himself when he performed the marriage ceremony for Frederick and Anna "Johnson" Douglass. Author of numerous books, articles, and sermons, he was selected as a delegate to the 1843 World's Antislavery Convention and the World's Peace Convention, both held in London.

Courtesy of Documenting the American South, the University of North Carolina at Chapel Hill Libraries

by Sir Walter Scott, Nathan suggested the name *Douglas*, a noble character in the poem. Frederick appreciated the suggestion and chose *Douglass*, the common spelling of the name in his day.

So Frederick Augustus Washington Bailey, the name given by his mother when he was born, became Frederick Douglass, the name that would ring its way into history.

The first home of Frederick and Anna Douglass, New Bedford, Massachusetts.
Photo by author

Nathan and Mary (Polly) Johnson

Active abolitionists living in New Bedford, Nathan and Polly Johnson acquired several properties in the community. Nathan was elected president of the 1847 National Convention of Colored Citizens. By providing a home for him and guiding him on how to live as a freeman, Frederick Douglass said the Johnsons helped him "in this the hour of my extremest need."

Situated next to the first home of Frederick and Anna Douglass was this building, also owned by Nathan Johnson, a former Quaker meetinghouse for the New Bedford Society of Friends.
Photo by author

"A NEW NATION CONCEIVED IN LIBERTY . . ."

A Brand New Life

The very first afternoon after arriving in New Bedford, Massachusetts, Frederick Douglass walked down to the wharves. Having lived near shipyards and worked as a caulker on ships in Baltimore, he felt he was right at home. Yet the marked difference between his new home and his old stood out sharply in his mind.

Here on the wharves in New Bedford everyone was free. Workers quietly tended to their tasks, black and white together, fitting out the full-rigged whaling ships for long voyages to faraway seas. Nowhere could the slave driver's whip be heard. Absent were the mournful tunes of the slaves' work songs. Instead, everywhere it seemed, Douglass saw men and women clothed in the simple dress of Quakers, a group of people known to be abolitionists. He felt safe here and was eager to find work to support himself and his new wife.

Frederick Douglass, newly free. Mural in New Bedford, Massachusetts.
Photo by author

Within three days, Douglass found his first job loading barrels of oil on a sloop headed for New York. It was hard work. However, Douglass admitted, "That day's work I considered the real starting point of something like a new existence." For the first time in his life, the work and the wages he earned were his own.

Even though New Bedford was in Massachusetts, a free state, Douglass experienced deep prejudice. Threatened by white workers if he took a high-paying job such as caulking, Douglass put his hands to any work he could find. "I now prepared myself to do anything which came to hand in the way of turning an honest penny," Douglass explained, "sawed wood—dug cellars—shoveled coal—swept chimneys with Uncle Lucas Debuty—rolled oil casks on the wharves—helped

to load and unload vessels—worked in Ricketson's candle works—in Richmond's brass foundry, and elsewhere; and thus supported myself and family for three years."

One of the jobs Frederick Douglass found was as a servant in the home of attorney John H. Clifford, who would later become governor of Massachusetts. Here in this elegant mansion, one of Douglass's duties was to wait on important guests and serve them in the dining room. One of the guests he served was an aristocrat named Robert C. Winthrop. As Douglass stood behind Winthrop's chair, fulfilling his duties as servant, he was captivated by the elegant conversation of this wealthy and influential man. Douglass simply could not have imagined that 25 years later, he would share the same speaking platform

(left) Quilt: "Tote that Bale," by Barbara Pietila, 2006. *Photo by author, courtesy of Frederick Douglass–Isaac Myers Maritime Park*

(right) New Bedford home of John H. Clifford, where Douglass served as a servant. *Photo by author*

with Winthrop, scheduled to speak in the famous Faneuil Hall of Boston before a grand and brilliant audience.

That day would come. For now, however, newly freed from slavery, Douglass was happy to find work as a servant and earn his own wages.

A Growing Family

Frederick and Anna Douglass made New Bedford their home. For the first time in her life, Anna enjoyed taking care of her own home instead of working as a maid for someone else.

What a difference Frederick and Anna found in New Bedford! Unlike areas in the slave states where maids had to tote water from a well, New Bedford was home to a variety of up-to-date gadgets. Water was available inside the houses from indoor pumps. Kitchens had sinks and drains. The earliest manual washing machines were common in most households, although Anna probably still used a washboard when she first arrived in New Bedford.

The Douglasses started a family. Anna stayed at home in the two rooms they rented, caring for their growing family. First came Rosetta, a precious little girl. Next arrived a son, Lewis Henry. A second son followed, and they named him Frederick Douglass Jr., after his father.

Frederick and Anna fondly remembered these early years of their new life together. Each day, Frederick came home from a hard day's work to eat the meal Anna had prepared. Dinner dishes were spread out neatly on a snow-white

The Douglass Children

Frederick and Anna Douglass had five children. Their first three children were born in New Bedford, Massachusetts. Rosetta, their first daughter, was born in 1839. Lewis Henry, their oldest son, was born in 1840. They named their third child Frederick Jr. when he was born in 1842. Their fourth child was born in 1844 when they lived in Lynn, Massachusetts. This son was named Charles Remond after the most famous black abolitionist of the day before Douglass stepped into that role. Their last child, Annie, was born in 1849 after they moved to Rochester, New York, but died at a young age.

Toy trolley belonging to the Douglass grandchildren. *Photo by author, courtesy of Frederick Douglass–Isaac Myers Maritime Park*

These playing cards belonged to the Douglass grandchildren. *Photo by author, courtesy of Frederick Douglass–Isaac Myers Maritime Park*

CLOTHESPIN DOLLS

During the early years of America, many children played with dolls made from clothespins and fabric scraps. You can make clothespin dolls of the five Douglass children.

Materials

* Doll pins, or old-fashioned wooden clothespins without springs
* Craft paint
* Paint brush
* Fabric scraps
* Scissors
* Ruler or tape measure
* Fine-tip permanent markers

➥ Working on a covered surface, paint several wooden doll pins brown. Allow to dry. Cut various basic shapes from fabric with the measurements shown.

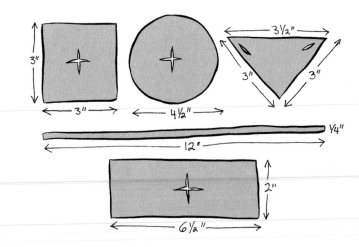

To cut a tiny slit for the neck or waist, follow Steps 1 to 3 as shown.

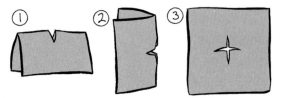

To make a clothespin doll of Lewis Douglass, paint the bottom half of a doll pin black to make it look like he is wearing black pants. Cut a slit in a 3-inch square and slip it over the head of the doll pin to form his shirt. Tie a ¼ x 12-inch fabric strip around his waist as shown to form a belt. Make dolls of Frederick Jr. and Charles in a similar way.

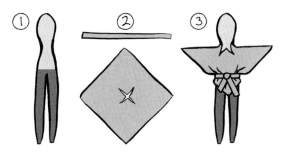

The clothespin dolls of Rosetta and Annie Douglass will wear a dress or a skirt and blouse. To make the skirt and blouse, cut a slit in a 4½-inch circle and slip it over the head of the doll pin, pulling it down to the waist. Cut a slit in a 3-inch square and slip it over the head of the doll pin to form her blouse. Tie a ¼ x 12-inch fabric strip around her waist as shown to form a belt.

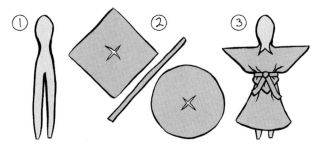

To make a dress, cut a slit in the 2 x 6½-inch rectangle and slip it over the head of the doll pin. Tie a ¼ x 12-inch fabric strip around her waist as shown to form a belt.

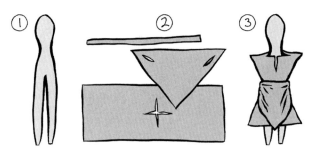

If you want to add an apron or a scarf, tie ¼ x 12-inch fabric strips through slits cut in a triangle as shown. Then tie the triangle at the waist to form an apron, or over the head to form a scarf. You may add shoes or facial features to your dolls with paints or permanent markers.

tablecloth. Their small children gathered around the table to join in the meal together. Even though surrounded by hardships and living in near-poverty conditions, it was a happy time for the young family. The joy of freedom made it so.

Joining the Church

Soon after arriving in New Bedford, Frederick Douglass decided to look for a church where he could worship. Believing firmly that men and women were created equal and should enjoy equal rights, he attended the Elm Street Methodist Church, a mostly white congregation. Upon his arrival, however, he was instructed to join the other free blacks seated upstairs in the gallery, apart from the main body of the congregation.

Douglass, unsure of the church's stand on equal rights, sat in the area where the church officials directed him to sit. After several meetings, however, it was time for the church to take communion, or the Lord's Supper. That day, after the minister preached his sermon, he invited the white members to join in the Lord's Supper. When they were finished, the minister then invited the black members to come forward to take communion. At this invitation, Douglass said, "I went *out*, and have never been in that church since, although I honestly went there with a view to joining that body."

Douglass felt greatly disappointed. Here, living as a free man in a free state, the deep prejudice he encountered caused him to struggle. How could people profess to be Christians and view another person with such deep prejudice

Indoor water pump in the home of Frederick and Anna Douglass at Cedar Hill.
Photo by author, courtesy National Park Service, Frederick Douglass National Historic Site

James Varick

Black Methodists in New York City organized to form a new denomination: African Methodist Episcopal Zion. In 1822 James Varick was elected as the first bishop. The A.M.E. Zion eventually became known as the Freedom Church because included among its lists of members were famous abolitionists such as Frederick Douglass, Harriet Tubman, and Sojourner Truth.

Courtesy of Documenting the American South, the University of North Carolina at Chapel Hill Libraries

simply because their skin was a different color? Douglass would wrestle with this conflict his entire life. After visiting several other churches in the community and being treated in the same degrading manner, Douglass finally joined the African Methodist Episcopal Zion (A.M.E. Zion) denomination, which had a small African American church in New Bedford.

Frederick Douglass quickly formed deep bonds of friendship with the members of the A.M.E. Zion church. Eager to strengthen his own faith and burning with a desire to speak about the life principles he was learning, he quickly became a class leader. He soon began preaching sermons as well. In this small church whose congregation met in a school building on Second Street, Douglass had his earliest experiences as a speaker. It was a time he always remembered with joy.

The *Liberator*

One day, about five months after moving to New Bedford, a young man offered Frederick Douglass a subscription to a newspaper. Douglass said, "I told him I had but just escaped from slavery, and was of course very poor, and remarked further, that I was unable to pay for it." Nevertheless, the young man signed Douglass up for a subscription and handed him his first copy of the *Liberator*.

The *Liberator* was an antislavery newspaper edited by William Lloyd Garrison. It took a firm stand against slavery and was read widely by abolitionists. "I not only liked," Frederick Douglass admitted, "I *loved* this paper, and its editor.

He seemed a match for all the opponents of emancipation."

Douglass devoured this newspaper as a starving man gulps down food. He read every issue from cover to cover. During this time Douglass worked at a brass foundry. His work involved high temperatures and extreme physical labor. He worked the bellows, swung the crane, and emptied containers where boiling metal was poured into different shapes. At times, Douglass worked around the clock, two days in a row, or he worked every single day of the workweek.

Having little spare time for reading, Douglass was determined to read the newspaper in whichever way he could. He frequently nailed the pages of the newspaper to a post near where he worked. While he pumped a heavy beam up and down to work the bellows at the foundry, with the furnace's heat blasting over him, he read the newspaper's articles. It breathed fire into his soul.

> "The *Liberator* was a paper after my own heart."
> —Frederick Douglass

For the first time, Douglass truly gained an understanding of what it meant to be an abolitionist. He learned about the abolitionist movement that was sweeping the northern United States, as well as England, gathering supporters who wanted to bring slavery to an end. He read articles written by famous abolitionists and grew familiar with their names, their passions, and their purpose. Above them all rose the voice of their staunch and fearless leader, William Lloyd Garrison.

Nantucket Antislavery Convention

Each week, Frederick Douglass read through the freshly printed pages of the *Liberator*'s current issue. Each time an antislavery meeting in New Bedford was announced, he attended with great interest. Douglass sat in the crowded rooms, intense with the desire to hear the words of the speakers denouncing slavery and its wicked practices. At these meetings, he listened. He learned. He applauded. But he was always just a member of the audience. Douglass admitted, "I had not

then dreamed of the possibility of my becoming a public advocate of the cause so deeply imbedded in my heart."

This was about to change.

During the summer months of 1841, plans were underway to hold a large antislavery convention in Nantucket. A nearby island off the shore of New Bedford, Nantucket was a prosperous whaling community that was home to many whalers or seafaring men, such as Absalom Boston, and their families.

Hearing about the upcoming abolitionist meeting, Frederick Douglass decided to attend. Since the day he had escaped from slavery three years earlier, he had not taken a rest. "The three years of my freedom," Douglass explained, "had been spent in the hard school of adversity." His hands were toughened by the constant work. He exhausted himself each day in rough and heavy

Absalom F. Boston (1785-1855)

Many African Americans worked in the whaling industry. During Frederick Douglass's time, one of the most prominent of the Nantucket whalers was Absalom Boston. A ship's captain who went on to become a wealthy businessman, Absalom Boston was active in politics and fought for the integration of Nantucket schools.

Courtesy of the Nantucket Historical Association, 1906.0056.001

labor. Douglass had devoted himself to earning a living to support his wife and children.

He decided to take a much-needed rest and go to the antislavery convention in Nantucket. There, among the crowd of a thousand men and women on August 11, 1841, Frederick Douglass felt his heart burning with the cause so many voices were speaking about—ending slavery. At that moment, he was singled out and approached by a very famous abolitionist named William Coffin.

Surprised that Coffin knew his name, Douglass learned that Coffin had attended his church in New Bedford. It was there that Coffin had heard Douglass preach. Now Coffin urged Douglass to speak here at the antislavery convention.

Frederick Douglass was shocked. He? A fugitive slave? Speak to a crowd with mostly whites in the audience? Unheard of! A fugitive slave had never done such a thing. Even at an antislavery convention!

Coffin insisted, however. He invited Douglass to step forward to the platform and speak a few words to the crowd.

Moved by the emotions that flooded his heart and inspired by the memories of his recent days of bondage, Douglass finally agreed. Overcome with excitement, he approached the platform and began to speak. "It was with the utmost difficulty that I could stand erect," he remembered, "or that I could command and articulate two words without hesitation and stammering. I trembled in every limb."

Yet speak he did. Instantly, something like a bolt of electricity shot through the crowd.

Douglass said, "The audience, though remarkably quiet before, became as much excited as myself."

A New Career

After Frederick Douglass finished his speech and stepped down from the platform, William Lloyd Garrison stood up to take his place. Stirred deeply by the testimony of Douglass regarding his life as a slave, Garrison declared, "Patrick Henry of revolutionary fame, never made a speech more eloquent in the cause of liberty, than the one we had just listened to from the lips of that hunted fugitive."

The crowd roared its approval. No fugitive had ever spoken before at a convention like this. Always before it had been white abolitionists or free blacks speaking out against slavery. For the first time in American history, a fugitive himself dared to speak up and describe what slavery was really like.

When that evening's thrilling program finally ended, Frederick Douglass was approached by yet another man. John Collins was the general agent of the Massachusetts Antislavery Society. Collins urged Douglass to join the society's ranks as a speaker.

Frederick Douglass refused. How could he support his family if he quit working and agreed to speak at antislavery conventions? How would he know what to say, uneducated as he was? But most importantly, how could he hide from Hugh Auld and escape the slave hunters if he agreed to become a public speaker? No. He could not work for the society.

John Collins insisted. No matter which objection Douglass raised, Collins would not listen. "Mr. Collins was not to be refused," Douglass admitted, "and I finally consented to go out for three months, supposing I should in that length of time come to the end of my story and my consequent usefulness."

William Lloyd Garrison
(1805-1879)

Great antislavery leader that he was, William Lloyd Garrison insisted his voice be heard, and he was. Best known as editor of the abolitionist newspaper the *Liberator*, his words were read by countless people in America as well as abroad. His passionate followers included Frederick Douglass, who was his friend, fellow speaker, and frequent traveling companion for many years.

From the collection of the Rochester Public Library Local History Division

A new day dawned in the life of Frederick Douglass. A new era began in the history of America.

A Holy Cause

The initial three months Frederick Douglass signed up to speak for the Massachusetts Antislavery Society quickly turned into a new career for this man who was still legally a slave. His master, Hugh Auld, still owned him and was still hunting Douglass, to capture him and return him to slavery. Like a whirlwind, Douglass swept through towns and villages across the northern states, speaking and enlisting members for the society. He often accompanied John Collins. Other well-known abolitionists frequently joined their meetings and shared the speaker's platforms with them. Because it was already his own passion, Frederick Douglass gave himself over completely to the great and holy cause of his new friends—to join together as one voice and bring an end to slavery.

During this time, William Lloyd Garrison became a mentor to Frederick Douglass. Now in frequent companionship with the editor of the *Liberator*, the paper that introduced Douglass to the abolitionist movement, Douglass hung on every word Garrison spoke. Douglass embraced Garrison's philosophy. Frederick Douglass himself became known as a Garrisonian, a member of the group of men and women who publicly approved of Garrison's passionate views on antislavery, women's rights, nonviolence, the church, and politics.

> "The cause was good, the men engaged in it were good, the means to attain its triumph, good."
> —Frederick Douglass

The admiration and respect Douglass held for Garrison were mirrored in Garrison's glowing support of Douglass. As editor of the *Liberator*, Garrison frequently published articles and speeches showcasing his new friend's rise to fame and influence. Everywhere Douglass spoke, people rose up to admire his testimony, his intelligence, and his powerful oratory skills. In his paper, Garrison frequently printed these words of praise and fervor over this new member among the ranks of abolitionists.

Room to Grow

In his first months of speaking with the Massachusetts Antislavery Society, Frederick Douglass simply shared his personal testimony of his life as a slave. He was careful, however, with the details he gave. "The only precaution I took," Douglass explained, "at the beginning, to prevent Master Thomas from knowing where I was, and what I was about, was the withholding my former name, my master's name, and the name of the state and county from which I came." Douglass was still a fugitive. His life was in danger. Slave hunters and kidnappers relentlessly searched the northern states to capture runaway slaves and return them to the South.

Quickly, however, Douglass needed room to grow. He grew bored repeating the same story night after night.

John Collins urged him to continue to repeat his testimony. "Let us have the facts, we will take care of the philosophy," Collins said.

People in the crowd repeated to Douglass, "Let us have the facts."

Even his close friend William Lloyd Garrison repeatedly whispered to him as he walked

Famous Orator

Everywhere he went, Frederick Douglass amazed listening audiences with his powerful voice and passionate message. Men and women sang his praises as one of the leading orators of the day.

Elizabeth Cady Stanton declared, "He stood there like an African prince, majestic in his wrath, as with wit, satire, and indignation he graphically described the bitterness of slavery and the humiliation of subjection."

A listener from Buffalo acknowledged, "I had never heard a fugitive slave speak, and was immensely interested to hear him. He rose, and I soon perceived he was all alive. His soul poured out with rare pathos and power."

In his *Sketches of Lynn*, author David Newhall Johnson stated, "He was more than six feet in height; and his majestic form, as he rose to speak, straight as an arrow, muscular, yet lithe and graceful, his flashing eye, and more than all, his voice, that rivaled Webster's in its richness, and in the depth and sonorousness of its cadences, made up such an ideal of an orator as the listeners never forgot."

SUGAR WATER

When Frederick Douglass visited a community and spoke, he sometimes lectured for hours at a time at several different meetings in the same day. At times his voice grew hoarse from so much speaking. To soothe his scratchy throat, he drank a simple remedy of sugar water.

In his autobiography, Douglass recalled a particularly trying day when he was scheduled to speak four times in one New England town. By the middle of the day, he was tired and hungry, yet no hotel would serve him and no home offered him its hospitality. Waiting for his last speaking engagement to begin, Douglass walked around the town in the chilly, drizzling rain of a New England northeaster. Seeing his predicament, a politician who was well known for his sentiments against abolitionists surprisingly invited Douglass into his home.

Aware that the senator's wife felt disturbed by his presence, Douglass said gently to her, "I have taken cold, and am hoarse from speaking, and I have found that nothing relieves me so readily as a little loaf sugar and cold water." He found that her demeanor softened. "With her own hands," Douglass remembered, "she brought me the water and sugar. I thanked her with genuine earnestness, and from that moment, I could see that her prejudices were more than half gone, and that I was more than half welcome at the fireside of this Democratic Senator."

Materials

* 1 cup cold water
* 1 tablespoon sugar
* Spoon

➤ Stir the sugar into the water with a spoon until it is dissolved. Drink the sweetened water slowly, allowing it to soothe your throat. Did it work?

up to the speaker's platform, "Tell your story, Frederick."

However, Frederick Douglass could not go on just simply describing the wrongs he had experienced as a slave. "I could not always obey," he explained, "for I was now reading and thinking. New views of the subject were presented to my mind. It did not entirely satisfy me to *narrate* wrongs; I felt like *denouncing* them."

New Companions

As Frederick Douglass grew in his ability to speak out against the evils of slavery, his circle of friends and companions also widened. During his first years of speaking on the lecture circuit, he was often seen with greats such as William Lloyd Garrison, Wendell Phillips, Samuel J. May, and Charles Lenox Remond. A singing group, the Hutchinson family, toured with them. The Hutchinsons provided music at the meetings, stirring the crowd to join in by singing popular antislavery songs as well as songs the Hutchinsons wrote.

As he traveled back and forth to attend his many different speaking engagements, Frederick Douglass made it his personal duty to bring an end to segregation, the practice of separating blacks from whites. For example, he was determined to do all he could to help end segregation on the Eastern Railroad.

Douglass used the railroad frequently. The Eastern Railroad had been a source of much trouble to its passengers by forcing blacks to ride separately in a "Jim Crow" car, or train car where blacks had to ride. The railroad had been written up in various publications, including the *Liberator*, for how its conductors and brakemen bullied African American passengers and forced them to move from their seats to the degrading car at the back of the train. Not only was it humiliating for blacks to be separated from other passengers, but the accommodations in the Jim Crow car were not as nice as those in the rest of the train.

One day Frederick Douglass bought a ticket and sat down in a seat on the train. When the conductor noticed Douglass, he ordered Douglass to leave. Douglass calmly replied that he liked the seat he had chosen and didn't care to move. With this, the conductor called several brakemen to come. Frederick Douglass reported with a note of humor he often displayed, "When they took hold of me, I felt my hands instinctively clutch the arms of the seat where I sat, and I seemed to be very firmly attached to the place." To remove Douglass, the brakemen had to lift him up and carry him off, seat and all.

> "I have neither been miserable because of the ill-feeling of those about me, nor indifferent to popular approval, and I think, upon the whole, I have passed a tolerably cheerful and even joyful life." —Frederick Douglass

After this incident, the Eastern Railroad refused to stop at Douglass's hometown of Lynn, Massachusetts, for several days. But so many people protested, and Douglass continued to fight so diligently, that eventually the Eastern Railroad stopped this practice. Blacks and whites could then travel through Massachusetts by train as equals.

Charles Lenox Remond (1810–1873)

Before Frederick Douglass escaped from slavery, Charles Lenox Remond was the most famous African American orator of his day. Remond was a Garrisonian. A staunch abolitionist, he became the first black hired as a speaker for the American Antislavery Society. In 1840 this organization selected Remond as one of its delegates to the World's Antislavery Convention in London.

Remond and Douglass frequently traveled together and often shared the speaker's platform in their commitment to help bring slavery to an end. Remond's sister, Sarah Parker Remond, was also a well-known abolitionist of the day.

Courtesy of the Boston Public Library, Print Department

Forerunner of the American Civil Rights Movement

One hundred years before Rosa Parks helped start the civil rights movement by refusing to move from her seat on a bus in Montgomery, Alabama, Frederick Douglass fought against segregation everywhere he went. He sat down in the front seats on trains, joined the dining tables on steamships, and attempted—many times successfully—to help integrate transportation systems wherever he traveled. One time when Douglass, riding unnoticed inside a streetcar, observed that a black man was being ordered off at the other end of the car, he called out, "Go on! Let the gentleman alone! No one here objects to his riding."

Frederick Douglass sat down in segregated restaurants. He joined boycotts of establishments that treated blacks unfairly. After the Free Soil Convention in 1852, a local hotel prepared dinner for 300 guests but would not allow African Americans to eat in its restaurant. All the delegates from the convention joined Douglass in a boycott and dined at a different hotel. He also worked successfully to integrate public schools in his area.

At one time, upon meeting a man who displayed obvious prejudice, Douglass said, "I suspected his trouble was colorphobia, and, though I regretted his malady, I knew his case was not necessarily dangerous, and I was not without some confidence in my skill and ability in healing diseases of that type." His brave and heroic efforts set the stage for the American civil rights movement over 100 years later.

The Latimer Case

It was during this time that news from Boston reached the ears of Frederick Douglass and his speaking companions. In October 1842 Frederick Douglass joined with Charles Remond and others to speak to audiences around the clock against the arrest and imprisonment of a fugitive named George Latimer. The reason for his arrest? Documents had been produced stating that Latimer was the runaway slave of a man in Virginia.

Latimer was locked in a Boston jail. Douglass and Remond insisted this was an outrage! How could fugitives or free blacks be safe in the state of Massachusetts as long as incidents like this were allowed to take place? Massachusetts wasn't a slave state in the Deep South, yet its officials and its jails were aiding in the capture of slaves.

Douglass and Remond were swept up in the tide of abolitionist fervor. Their tireless efforts were not in vain. Money was raised and arrangements were made to purchase George Latimer's freedom. He was set free. A petition was written, signed by 65,000 outraged citizens, and submitted to the Massachusetts government. A new law was passed, stating that Massachusetts state jails and state officials were no longer allowed to play a part in the capture of runaway slaves.

Hundred Conventions

A grand idea ignited the abolitionist fire to its most heroic efforts yet. With the victory of the Latimer case burning in their souls, the plan for a "Hundred Conventions" tour rocked the North and was soon set in motion. State by state, county by county, town by town, the goal of the Hundred Conventions was to reach every northern community in the hope of enlisting supporters for the antislavery movement. Frederick Douglass and Charles Lenox Remond embarked for the tour across the northern states along with several other small groups of speakers. The plan was to travel individually or in pairs, regrouping from time to time, and meeting up together for exciting and glorious events at key locations.

The six-month tour was grueling. The men never knew if they would be met with crowds eager to hear their words or by mobs bent on violence. At times Douglass and Remond traveled together. At other times, the two men were joined by another speaker. And still other times, Douglass traveled and spoke alone.

Douglass, Remond, and the other men traveled and spoke all across the North including Massachusetts, Vermont, and into New York.

While in New York, Douglass and Remond attended the National Convention of Colored Citizens. A fiery radical, Reverend Henry Highland Garnet, spoke at the convention urging slaves to revolt and be willing to fight and shed blood if necessary. Frederick Douglass and Charles Lenox Remond, both supporters of William

George Latimer (c. 1819–c. 1900)

The arrest and imprisonment of George Latimer united abolitionists in this 1842 landmark case for freedom. Douglass and others like him argued for the freedom of this fugitive . . . and won. The result? A new law was passed in Massachusetts forbidding state jails or state officials to be instrumental in the recapture of runaway slaves.

After being set free, George Latimer and his fugitive wife joined the antislavery campaign. They started a family. Their son, Lewis H. Latimer, grew up to become a member of the Edison Pioneers, a prestigious group of inventors who worked with Thomas Edison.

Henry Highland Garnet (1815–1882)

As a youth, Henry Highland Garnet experienced various instances of racial violence. An ordained minister, he used the pulpit, the pen, and the speaker's platform to call Americans to fight to bring an end to slavery.

Frederick Douglass initially opposed Garnet, siding with the Garrisonians. However, as the government's grip tightened more firmly and took away more and more of their rights, abolitionists such as Douglass began to support Garnet's radical views.

Courtesy of Documenting the American South, the University of North Carolina at Chapel Hill Libraries

CARPETBAG

As did most people of his day, Frederick Douglass carried a carpetbag on his travels. Inside were his personal items and essentials for the trip. A sturdy type of suitcase, carpetbags were made from real carpet.

Materials

* Newspaper
* Craft scissors
* Ruler or measuring tape
* 1 yard 56-inch-wide heavy upholstery fabric
* Fabric scissors
* Yardstick
* Pencil or chalk
* Safety pins or straight pins
* Sewing machine
* Thread
* Pair of bamboo oval purse handles, 8½ x 5½ inches (or similar handles)

Adult supervision required

➡ Cut a 16 x 20-inch rectangle from newspaper. This will be the pattern you use.

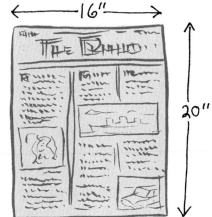

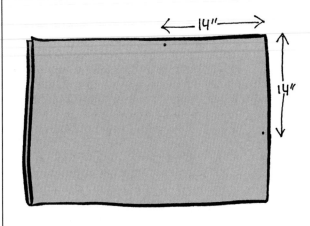

Fold the upholstery fabric in half, right sides together, to measure 1 yard by 28 inches. Use the fabric scissors to trim or cut away the selvage, or unfinished edge, of the fabric.

Starting at the right corner of the fabric (not the corner that is on a fold), measure 14 inches from both sides, and mark a dot with a pencil or chalk.

Place the newspaper pattern on the fabric so that the two corners are on the two dots. Draw a dashed line around three sides of the newspaper on the fabric. Use the fabric scissors to cut along the dotted lines through both pieces of fabric.

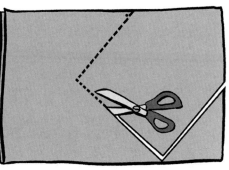

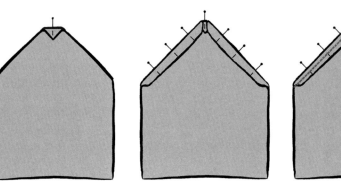

Prepare both pieces of fabric in the following way:

Fold 1½ inches of the point right side over to the underside of the fabric. Pin in place. Fold the right side over to the underside ½ inch along the edges on both sides of the point. Hold in place with safety pins or straight pins. Using the sewing machine, sew both these edges and the folded point to lie flat.

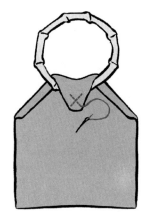

Fold the finished point 5½ inches down, over the handle, right side over to the underside. Stitch an X near the point to hold the handle in place.

Sew both pieces of prepared fabric together along the sides and bottom, right sides together. Turn the bag right side out. Carry your carpetbag by the handles for a sturdy tote.

The Philadelphia Vigilance Committee included Thomas Garrett, Robert Purvis (middle row, right), William Still (bottom row, right), Passmore Williamson, N. W. Depee, Melloe McKim, James Miller, Jacob White, and Charles Wise.
Courtesy of the Boston Public Library, Print Department

Lloyd Garrison's philosophy of using persuasion rather than violence to end slavery, were directly opposed to Garnet's viewpoints. Douglass took his turn lecturing, passionately expressing his nonviolent views in direct contrast to Garnet's.

After the convention was over in New York, Douglass continued to speak in states such as Ohio, Indiana, and Pennsylvania. The final stop of the tour for Douglass and his companions was in Philadelphia during December for the 10th anniversary celebration of the American Antislavery Society. Robert Purvis, vice president of the society and leader among the black abolitionists in Philadelphia, led the ceremonies.

In spite of the troubles they frequently encountered from mob violence or hardships they experienced along the road, the Hundred Conventions was declared a success. In an era when communication was difficult and travel was hard, Douglass and his fellow lecturers had reached the northern states with their antislavery message.

Questioning His Past

By now, Frederick Douglass had become a polished and powerful orator. He read constantly. The education he received from books and newspapers influenced his lectures. His speeches rang out across the northern states and persuaded countless numbers to join the abolitionist cause. He dominated the speaker's platform. People often came to meetings just to hear him speak and left as soon as he was done, even if the meeting was not yet over.

Robert Purvis (1810-1898)

Because of his work organizing the Philadelphia Vigilance Committee, Robert Purvis became known as the Father of the Underground Railroad. He was rich, and he looked white. However, his grandmother had been a slave, putting him under the full legal restrictions of US law denying African Americans their rights.

Purvis was close friends with his father-in-law, wealthy African American sail maker James Forten from Philadelphia. Together they championed equal rights, were active in many antislavery and reform groups, and fought for equal education and women's rights. Robert Purvis's wife, Harriet, was active in leadership roles and the antislavery cause as well. Their home was a stop on the Underground Railroad.

Courtesy of the Boston Public Library, Print Department

And then it happened. People began to doubt that this famous, educated, and polished speaker ever could have been a slave. They thought he was an imposter! Frederick Douglass heard the people in the audience whisper as he walked past them on his way to the podium, "He's never been a slave, I'll warrant ye."

The day had come. It was time for Frederick Douglass to throw off the veil he was hiding behind. It was time for him to tell the truth about his real name, his birthplace, and the name of his owners.

At the peril of death, Frederick Douglass decided to write his autobiography.

~ 4 ~

"DEDICATED TO THE PROPOSITION THAT ALL MEN ARE CREATED EQUAL . . ."

New Heights of Achievement

Frederick Douglass, famous orator, was very different from Frederick Augustus Washington Bailey, slave. The four years spent in freedom had transformed him. Yes, he was still the same person, but Frederick Douglass spread his wings as a free man and flew to heights never before thought possible for a former slave.

He was educated now, through the books and newspapers he read and the company he kept. He was a powerful speaker, his skills at debate sharpened with the passion for his cause. He was famous and had many influential friends, a key player in the whirlwind of the abolitionist movement that was sweeping across the northern United States, making its presence known among the slaveholders and in the slave cabins in the Deep South and blowing across the Atlantic to the ears of sympathetic listeners in Great Britain.

Stepping back from the speaking circuit, Frederick Douglass spent 1844 to 1845 focused on writing his autobiography. He decided to tell the truth about his identity, the identity of the men and women who owned him, and the names of the places he lived and worked as a slave.

This was a dangerous step. He was a fugitive, hiding from those who were looking to capture him and return him to his owner, Thomas Auld. After all, a young, strong man in his prime was a valuable piece of property—worth over $700, a considerable amount of money in those days. Kidnappers and slave hunters itched with greed to collect payment on his capture.

On one hand, Douglass had many close and influential friends who would fight against anyone who dared try to capture him. He shared, "It is not probable that any open attempt to secure me as a slave could have succeeded, further than the obtainment, by my master, of the money value of my bones and sinews. Fortunately for me, in the four years of my labors in the abolition cause, I had gained many friends, who would have suffered themselves to be taxed to almost any extent to save me from slavery."

On the other hand, however, the possibility of recapture was very, very real. "I was constantly in danger," Douglass admitted, "of being spirited away, at a moment when my friends could render me no assistance. In traveling about from place to place—often alone—I was much exposed to this sort of attack."

Still a Secret

In his autobiography, however, there was one detail of his life that Frederick Douglass determined would yet remain a secret. He refused to tell the details of his escape. Uncomplicated as it was, he did not want to destroy the opportunity for other slaves to do as he did. He knew it was a common practice among slaves to dress like a sailor, borrow a sailor's protection papers, and escape by train, steamboat, and carriage from the South to the North.

The Upper-Ground Railroad

During the years leading up to the Civil War, it became popular for fugitives to publish their successful escapes. Frederick Douglass called this the *Upper-ground Railroad*. He never told the details of his escape until after the end of the Civil War. In his autobiography, he explained why:

> I have never approved of the very public manner, in which some of our western friends have conducted what *they* call the *"Underground Railroad,"* but which, I think, by their open declarations, has been made, most emphatically, the *"Upper-ground Railroad."* Its stations are far better known to the slaveholders than to the slaves. . . . We owe something to the slaves, south of Mason and Dixon's line, as well as to those north of it; and, in discharging the duty of aiding the latter, on their way to freedom, we should be careful to do nothing which would be likely to hinder the former, in making their escape from slavery.

This was a common practice whispered from one slave to another, but it was not publicly known among slaveholders. Yes, slave owners and officials in southern states *suspected* this type of thing. Papers were checked carefully on every train or boat heading north. But these were only suspicions. If Douglass had shared in his autobiography that he had successfully escaped using this method, it then would have been *impossible* for any other slave to try it. Douglass decided never to tell his secret or explain the details about his escape as long as slavery still existed in America.

His Narrative Published

After Frederick Douglass finished writing his autobiography, he showed it to his closest friends. They were concerned that publishing his manuscript would put him in extreme danger. Douglass said, "My true friends, Mr. Garrison and Mr. Phillips, had no faith in the power of Massachusetts to protect me in my right to liberty."

After reading Douglass's manuscript, Wendell Phillips cautioned Frederick Douglass. "Mr.

Famous Escapes

Ellen and William Craft escaped together. Ellen, who was light-skinned, disguised herself as a sick, wealthy southern white man traveling north. Her husband, William, pretended to be a slave attending the young "gentleman." They took public transportation and successfully traveled openly in their disguise.

Ellen Craft
Courtesy of Documenting the American South, the University of North Carolina at Chapel Hill Libraries

The "Saltwater Slave" held onto a steamboat, washed by the waves of the sea for three days and nights in his hiding place. The boat landed on free soil in a northern port, and he was free.

Courtesy of Documenting the American South, the University of North Carolina at Chapel Hill Libraries

Henry "Box" Brown hid inside a wooden crate. A friend mailed the box to an abolitionist living in a northern state. This cartoon shows Frederick Douglass, second from left, helping to open the box.

Abolitionists (left to right) Wendell Phillips, William Lloyd Garrison, and George Thompson.
Courtesy of the Boston Public Library, Print Department

"Sincerely and earnestly hoping that this little book may do something toward throwing light on the American slave system and hastening the glad day of deliverance to the millions of my brethren in bonds—faithfully relying upon the power of truth, love, and justice, for success in my humble efforts—and solemnly pledging my self anew to the sacred cause, —I subscribe myself."

—Frederick Douglass, Lynn, Massachusetts, April 28, 1845

Phillips, especially," Douglass explained, "considered me in danger, and said, when I showed him the manuscript of my story, if in my place, he would throw it into the fire."

It was a risk, however, that Douglass decided to take. In 1845 he published his first autobiography, *Narrative of the Life of Frederick Douglass, an American Slave, Written by Himself.* In the front of his book, he included a preface written by William Lloyd Garrison and a letter from Wendell Phillips.

Fleeing from Danger

After publishing his *Narrative*, Frederick Douglass moved his family from New Bedford to Lynn, Massachusetts. Anna and Frederick settled into the pretty cottage they built. Their son Charles Remond was born. By now, their oldest daughter, Rosetta, was six years old.

Just as their life was beginning in their new surroundings, however, dark storm clouds gathered overhead. Slaveholders throughout the South expressed their furious reaction to the *Narrative*. Now the truth about Frederick Douglass was known. Slave hunters and kidnappers could trace his whereabouts. His life was in grave danger. Even Anna, who had helped in his escape, was in danger because she had aided a fugitive.

It was an anxious time. His friends urged Douglass to flee the country. How could he, though? His wife and four children would be left alone—unprotected and unprovided for!

Friends rallied around for support. Abigail and Lydia Mott, cousins of famed women's rights activist Lucretia Mott, invited young Rosetta into their home to watch over her and ease Anna's burden of caring alone for the children.

Anna found work binding shoes to bring in an income while raising the children alone.

Their many friends in the Antislavery Societies of Lynn and Boston promised to help Frederick and Anna in any way they could. They promised to guard the family while Douglass was away.

"Flee!" friends urged Douglass from all sides. "Go now, before it's too late!"

And so it was with a heavy and anxious heart that Frederick Douglass said good-bye to Anna and his four children, booked passage on a steamer to England, and sailed across the Atlantic to live in safety, out of reach of the men who wanted to capture him and sentence him back into life—or death—as a slave.

An Anxious Time

True to their word, the friends in the Antislavery Societies of Lynn and Boston helped Anna and the children during the anxious years while Frederick Douglass was away from home. They invited Anna to the weekly meetings of a ladies' sewing circle that prepared items to sell during the annual Antislavery Fair held in Faneuil Hall in Boston. Prior to each meeting, the other women from Lynn came to the Douglass house and helped complete that day's household responsibilities so Anna could be free to come in the afternoon.

Anna was an active member in various societies. Her daughter Rosetta later recalled that "no circle was felt to be complete without her presence." During these years, Anna was in charge of a committee of women who provided the refreshments for the sewing circle.

With limited financial resources, Anna managed to keep the household free from debt during her husband's entire absence. From England, Frederick Douglass sent home money whenever he could. Anna also set aside a certain amount of money from her income from binding shoes and regularly donated these precious dollars to the Antislavery Societies. Regarding Anna's great skill in managing the family's finances, daughter Rosetta later said, "I have often heard my father speak in admiration of mother's executive ability."

Twenty-One Months Abroad

From 1845 to 1846 Frederick Douglass stayed in Great Britain for a total of 21 months, nearly two full years. Upon arriving in Liverpool, he became an instant celebrity and was greeted by many throughout the United Kingdom.

He hadn't planned for such a widespread reception. While traveling to Great Britain on the steamer across the Atlantic, however, he had been threatened by a mob of fellow passengers from New Orleans and Georgia. Enraged that Douglass was on board the steamboat and enjoying nearly equal privileges as they, they had declared they would throw him overboard. Their words caused the captain to threaten to lock this mob in chains.

Upon landing, these men headed directly to the English newspapers and published a story about their anger at a fugitive who dared enjoy equal privileges as they had. The result was that every abolitionist in England (and there were many) heard the news that the famous orator, Frederick Douglass, had arrived in their country, and they welcomed him with open arms.

During the next two years, Frederick Douglass traveled throughout England, Ireland, Scotland, and Wales. He said, "I visited and lectured in nearly all the large towns and cities in the United Kingdom, and enjoyed many favorable opportunities for observation and information."

At times while in Great Britain, Frederick Douglass traveled alone. At other times, he was in the company of American friends such as William Lloyd Garrison. And everywhere he went, he was treated as an equal with no regard to the color of his skin. What a shock this was! Douglass was so moved by the striking difference during his stay in England from his daily life in America that he remarked:

> The spirit of freedom that seems to animate all with whom I come in contact, and the entire absence of everything that looked like prejudice against me, on account of the color of my skin—contrasted so strongly with my long and

bitter experience in the United States, that I look with wonder and amazement on the transition.

Frederick Douglass had entered a different world when he landed on Great Britain's soil. He discovered a world of equal rights that he liked very much. Regarding the people he met, Douglass noted, "They measure and esteem men according to their moral and intellectual worth, and not according to the color of their skin."

> **"I can truly say, I have spent some of the happiest moments of my life since landing in this country." —Frederick Douglass**

Longing for Anna and the children, for a brief time Douglass seriously considered moving his family to England. His new friends would have helped him settle there permanently. Weighing everything in his mind, though, he made his decision. "To this, however, I could not consent. I felt that I had a duty to perform—and that was, to labor and suffer with the oppressed in my native land." He decided to return to America.

No Longer a Fugitive

Something unexpected happened while Frederick Douglass was in England. Ellen Richardson, a Quaker, along with her sister-in-law, raised money to purchase his freedom. They communicated through various means with the Aulds in Maryland, who agreed to sell Frederick Douglass his freedom for a total of 150 pounds sterling, or more than $700.

The money was raised and papers were signed. Frederick Douglass was no longer a fugitive. He was a free man, ready to return home to the United States.

His new friends were not finished, however. More money was raised and Douglass was presented with a gift of nearly $2,500. What would he do with these funds? Start, publish, and edit a newspaper as his friends hoped he would.

In his discussions with his British friends, Douglass shared,

I further stated that, in my judgment, a tolerably well conducted press, in the hands of persons of the despised race, by calling out the mental energies of the race itself; by making them acquainted with their own latent powers; by enkindling among them the hope that for them there is a future; by developing their moral powers; by combining and reflecting their talents—would prove a most powerful means of removing prejudice, and of awakening an interest in them.

Frederick Douglass went on to explain to his friends that currently, "There was not, in the United States, a single newspaper regularly published by the colored people; that many attempts had been made to establish such papers; but that, up to that time, they had all failed."

With the money in his pocket for purchasing a printing press, Frederick Douglass booked passage for the United States on the same steamer he had first traveled across the Atlantic two years earlier. When he arrived at the boat, however, he was ordered to stay in a certain part of the ship. He was also told he would not be allowed to join the other passengers in the dining area. Douglass admitted, "For the first time in the many months spent abroad, I was met with proscription on account of my color."

Frederick Douglass was leaving the United Kingdom. He set his heart for home, and the battle ahead.

Hard Times

Frederick Douglass knew he would face great trials when he returned home to fight against slavery. He had not anticipated, however, that one of these trials would come from his closest friends.

William Lloyd Garrison and others told Douglass quite frankly that publishing a new newspaper would be a waste of time. They counseled him against starting the newspaper due to the fact Douglass never had a formal education.

This was very distressing for Douglass. His closest friends spoke strongly against the newspaper. "Nevertheless," Douglass stated, "I persevered. I felt that the want of education, great as it was, could be overcome by study, and that wisdom would come by experience." Douglass

Gerrit Smith helped fund Frederick Douglass's newspapers. Smith once told Douglass, "It is your mission to break down the walls of separation between the two races." *Courtesy of the Boston Public Library, Print Department*

SPREAD THE WORD ON BLACK ABOLITIONISTS

➥ Frederick Douglass was acquainted with almost every black abolitionist of his day. You can learn more about these American heroes and tell others about their significant contributions to our nation's history. One way to do this is to research and read about one or more of these important men and women who lived during the years leading up to the Civil War. Explore their impact on history in *Black Abolitionists* by Benjamin Quarles (Da Capo Press, 1969). Read their autobiographies or biographies, many of which can be found online. Look up their names in encyclopedias such as the *African American National Biography* by Henry Louis Gates Jr. and Evelyn Brooks Higginbotham (Oxford University Press, 2008).

After you have done your research, write an article about their important contributions to America and submit it to the community magazine or newspaper where you live. Perhaps it will get published and more people will learn about the lives of these famous black abolitionists.

Look up the person you researched on Wikipedia at www.wikipedia.org. If there isn't yet an entry about that person, write one and post it with the help of an adult. If there already is an entry about the person you researched, try to add at least one more fact to the encyclopedia article.

For a list of names of black abolitionists look at the website www.frederickdouglass.wordpress.com/black-abolitionists/. Here is a partial list to help you get started:

* William Wells Brown
* Mary Ann Shadd Cary
* Alexander Crummell
* Martin R. Delany
* Robert Forten
* Henry Highland Garnet
* Charlotte Forten Grimké

* Francis Grimké
* Nathan and Polly Johnson
* Jermain W. Loguen
* William Cooper Nell
* Harriet Forten Purvis
* Robert Purvis
* Charles Lenox Remond

* Sarah Parker Remond
* David Ruggles
* James McCune Smith
* Sojourner Truth
* Harriet Tubman
* William Whipper

believed that a newspaper published and edited by African Americans would help speed slavery to an end.

After much thought, Douglass decided to move away from Boston, where his friends' newspapers circulated. Frederick and Anna packed their bags and moved their family far away to Rochester, New York, where no abolitionist paper was yet published.

The move was hard for the Douglass family, especially for Anna. She left behind her close circle of friends as well as her active role in abolitionist groups. The city of Rochester did not welcome these trailblazers. Far away from the ideals of freedom found in Boston, the prejudice against free blacks was very strong in this northern city.

As their daughter Rosetta explained, "Prejudice in the early [18]40s in Rochester ran rampant and mother became more distrustful." In spite of these difficulties, however, Anna devoted her life to the abolitionist cause more than ever. Rosetta said, "Her life in Rochester was not less active in the cause of the slave, if anything she was more self-sacrificing."

The North Star

Frederick and Anna Douglass settled into their new home in spite of the difficulties. A newspaper office was set up in the heart of Rochester, two miles from their house. The *North Star* was chosen as the name of the newspaper, symbolic of the star many fugitives followed at night in their journey north to freedom. "Publication day was

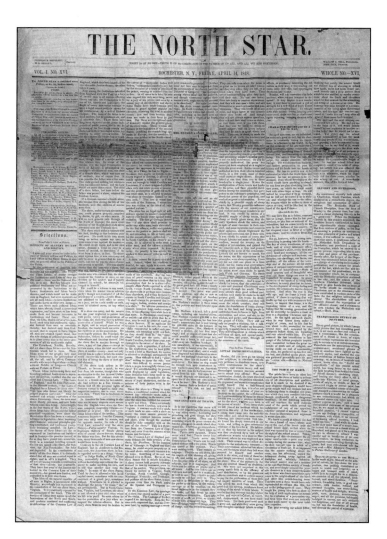

Frederick Douglass's famous newspaper, the *North Star*.
From the collection of the Rochester Public Library Local History Division

always a day for extra rejoicing," Rosetta shared, "as each weekly paper was felt to be another arrow sent on its way to do the work of puncturing the veil that shrouded a whole race in gloom."

The newspaper was a success. Finances were always a struggle, however, even though dedicated helpers such as Julia Griffiths worked tirelessly to raise financial support. Published every week, the newspaper had 3,000 to 4,000 faithful

William Cooper Nell
(1816–1874)

Growing up in Boston, William Cooper Nell started working for the *Liberator* at a young age. A strong supporter of William Lloyd Garrison, Nell joined Douglass in Rochester, bringing his many years of newspaper experience to the *North Star* as its first publisher. A prolific author, Nell wrote a book titled *The Colored Patriots of the American Revolution* that highlighted key contributions of African Americans during the Revolutionary War.

Frederick Douglass printed his newspaper, the *North Star,* in this office located in the Tallman Building on Main Street in Rochester. *From the collection of the Rochester Public Library Local History Division*

subscribers throughout America, Great Britain, and the West Indies.

Though it changed names several times, Douglass published his newspaper for nearly 20 years. He explained, "By one means or another I succeeded so well as to keep my pecuniary engagements, and to keep my antislavery banner steadily flying during all the conflict from the autumn of 1847 till the union of the states was assured and emancipation was a fact accomplished."

In the newspaper's earliest days, William Cooper Nell was listed as publisher of the *North Star*, Frederick Douglass as editor, and Martin R. Delany as assistant editor. The Douglass children helped set type, fold the papers for delivery, and accomplish other tasks in the office. Even Anna helped out on publication day each week, cooking delicious homemade biscuits and steaming stew to welcome home the weary workers. "Mother felt it her duty," their daughter Rosetta shared, "to have her table well supplied with extra provisions that day, a custom that we, childlike, fully appreciated. Our home was two miles from the center of the city, where our office was situated, and many times did we trudge through snow knee deep, as street cars were unknown."

Meeting a New Friend

Shortly after starting the *North Star*, Frederick Douglass received an invitation from John Brown to visit his home in Springfield, Massachusetts. Douglass had heard of this man before. His friends Henry Highland Garnet and Jermain W. Loguen had spoken of Brown with high regard. Eager to visit, Douglass willingly agreed to have dinner with this renowned and outspoken abolitionist.

John Brown and his family made Frederick Douglass feel at home. They served a simple stew called New England boiled dinner. After dinner, Brown sat down with Douglass and explained his reason for the invitation. John Brown denounced slavery with a vengeance. He said he did not believe it would ever end through political means or persuasive speeches.

John Brown
Courtesy of the Library of Congress,
LC-USZ62-89569

Martin Robison Delany (1812–1885)
Catherine A. Delany (1822–1894)

At times working with Frederick Douglass, and at other times associated with free blacks who settled in Liberia, Martin Delany promoted nationalism, black pride, and self-reliance. Before working with the *North Star*, Delany, who was a physician, published his own abolitionist newspaper in Pittsburgh, Pennsylvania, called the *Mystery*. His wife, Catherine, actively supported her husband in the antislavery cause.

Courtesy of Documenting the American South, the University of North Carolina at Chapel Hill Libraries

NEW ENGLAND BOILED DINNER

In Frederick Douglass's autobiography, he remembered the tasty meal he shared with John Brown and his family in their home. It was a simple meal but very flavorful and hearty.

Ingredients

* 1 corned beef brisket (2½ pounds)
* Large pot with cover
* Water
* Pepper to taste
* Salt to taste
* 3 white potatoes, cut into thick pieces
* 3 carrots, cut into thick slices
* 2 turnips, peeled and sliced into thick slices
* 1 onion, cut into thick pieces
* 1 cabbage, cut into 8 wedges

Adult supervision required

➡ Put the beef in the pot and cover it with water. Bring the water to a boil, then simmer with the salt and pepper for 2 hours or until the meat is tender. Add the vegetables to the pot and simmer for 30 minutes more, or until the vegetables are tender. Makes four 2-cup servings.

John Brown had a plan to snatch slaves from the plantations and set them free. It was a violent plan, and he shared the details with his guest. Frederick Douglass remembered that Brown said that "he had observed my course at home and abroad, and he wanted my cooperation."

Frederick Douglass admired John Brown's passion and leadership. After he returned home, that evening's visit haunted him. Over the days and months ahead, he wondered if John Brown was right. Would it take violent action to end slavery in America forever?

The Women's Rights Movement

Also during this time, another movement was rapidly gaining strength. Organized by such influential leaders as Elizabeth Cady Stanton, Lucretia Mott, and Susan B. Anthony, the women's rights movement took great strides toward achieving equal rights among men and women.

Always supporting equal rights among the races as well as among men and women, Frederick Douglass eagerly joined the cause. In July 1848 a convention was held in Seneca Falls, New York. Frederick Douglass advertised the convention in his newspaper and attended this landmark event.

A list of resolutions was created. Based on the Declaration of Independence, it was called the Declaration of Sentiments and proposed giving equal rights to women in a dozen areas. On one controversial issue, however, tempers ran high.

No one could agree to include in the declaration woman's suffrage, or allowing women the right to vote. Frederick Douglass stepped forward to the speaker's platform and spoke in defense of giving women the vote.

Speaking with his passion for this cause, Frederick Douglass declared to his audience, "Many who have at last made the discovery that the Negroes have some rights as well as other members of the human family, have yet to be convinced that women are entitled to any." He went on to state, "Standing as we do upon the watchtower of human freedom, we cannot be deterred from an expression of our approbation of any movement, however humble, to improve and elevate the character of any members of the human family." His speech ended with a powerful challenge, "There can be no reason in the world for denying to woman the exercise of the elective franchise, or a hand in making and administering the laws of the land."

As a result of Douglass's passionate and impromptu speech, a narrow majority agreed to include a woman's right to vote in the Declaration of Sentiments. The resolution passed.

A National Crisis

In 1850 there was a crisis so sudden and so shocking that it rocked the entire nation. A new law was passed as part of the Compromise of 1850. This law, the Fugitive Slave Act, affected Frederick Douglass and the free blacks living in America, changing their lives in countless ways.

Marble statue of three suffragists by Adelaide Johnson in the Capitol crypt, Washington, DC (left to right): Elizabeth Cady Stanton, Susan B. Anthony, Lucretia Mott. *Courtesy of the Library of Congress, LC-USA7-27850*

In essence, the Fugitive Slave Law declared, "No trial by jury for fugitives!" "No fugitive may testify in his own defense!" "One white man's word is all it takes to send a supposed fugitive into slavery!"

The lives of many men, women, and children throughout the northern states were in danger as never before. Countless fugitives had settled successfully in the North. Now they were no longer safe even in their own beds at night. Any black person—fugitive or not—could be arrested, claimed to be a runaway slave, then sent down South without a fair trial.

Large numbers of African Americans abandoned all hope in America and fled to Canada. Even many men and women who were not fugitives but were legally free citizens of the United States moved their families to Canada. Why? Because the Fugitive Slave Law was so powerful, slave hunters could kidnap their children and whisk them away into slavery without legal protection or help. Couples such as Martin and Catherine Delany moved to Canada where they felt they could raise their children in safety. Disillusioned and distraught, many people found it hard to believe that their nation's government could allow such an outrage.

Frederick Douglass, however, decided to stay and fight the battle, even though it waged

HOST AN ORATORICAL CONTEST

➡ Frederick Douglass was a brilliant orator, one of the most famous in American history. The speeches and lectures he gave, many without notes, thrilled the hearts of his audiences and still ring a clear message in support of civil rights today.

Familiarize yourself with many of Frederick Douglass's speeches and letters by reading Philip S. Foner's book, *Frederick Douglass: Selected Speeches and Writings*, abridged and adapted by Yuval Taylor (Lawrence Hill Books, 1999). Practice reading Douglass's speech on "The Rights of Women" from the July 28, 1848, edition of the *North Star*. (In Foner and Taylor's book, you'll find a copy of the speech Douglass gave at the Seneca Falls Convention.)

You can host an oratorical contest in your neighborhood, your classroom, or your community. Schedule a date when the contest will be held. Find a location that has a stage where each person can speak. Ask volunteers to be judges for the event, and award prizes.

Invite participants to each select one of Frederick Douglass's speeches to practice. Each orator should memorize the words of his or her speech and practice saying them out loud.

If you live near Washington, DC, sign up to join the Frederick Douglass Oratorical Contest hosted by the National Park Service at his home. For more information, visit www.nps.gov/frdo/forkids/oratorical-contest.htm.

stronger than ever. He denounced a government that would make decisions such as this. He traveled far and wide, delivering fiery speeches in defense of freedom.

He took an active role in the Vigilant Committees that were organized throughout the North. Frederick and Anna Douglass set up their home as an official stop on the Underground Railroad.

A Decisive Split

For the first four years after starting publication of the *North Star,* Frederick Douglass remained a staunch Garrisonian, firmly supporting William Lloyd Garrison and his views. Gradually, however, new ideas began to take shape.

His involvement in the women's rights movement and his association with John Brown helped influence this new way of thinking. He became disillusioned with the hope of peacefully bringing an end to slavery after the Fugitive Slave Act was brought into law. Another factor, however, was that in publishing the *North Star,* Frederick Douglass read and studied many important documents and books.

One of the documents he decided to study was the Constitution of the United States. Previously following Garrison's teaching that the Constitution was a pro-slavery document and therefore men should not vote during elections, Frederick Douglass now read the actual wording of the Constitution himself. He reached an entirely opposite conclusion. Douglass decided that instead of being pro-slavery, the principles

On the Question of the Constitution

Frederick Douglass split from the Garrisonian philosophy that Americans should not vote because they opposed the US Constitution as an unsound document. In his own words, Douglass explained his newly formed position:

After a time, a careful reconsideration of the subject convinced me that there was no necessity for dissolving the union between the northern and southern states, that to seek this dissolution was no part of my duty as an abolitionist, that to abstain from voting was to refuse to exercise a legitimate and powerful means for abolishing slavery, and that the Constitution of the United States not only contained no guarantees in favor of slavery, but, on the contrary, was in its letter and spirit an antislavery instrument, demanding the abolition of slavery as a condition of its own existence as the supreme law of the land.

in the Constitution did not support slavery at all! And therefore, as a free citizen of the United States, it was his duty and privilege to vote.

In 1851 Frederick Douglass officially broke away from William Lloyd Garrison and his followers. Douglass established new friendships, however, with men and women who supported his new views.

He continued his commitment to the antislavery cause. On July 5, 1852, he delivered his fiery and controversial speech, "What to the Slave Is the Fourth of July?" Standing before an attentive audience at Corinthian Hall in Rochester,

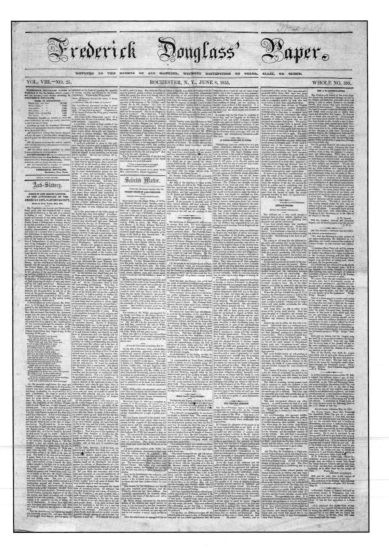

Frederick Douglass changed the name of his newspaper several times, including this version, *Frederick Douglass' Paper.* *From the collection of the Rochester Public Library Local History Division*

My Bondage and My Freedom. In this edition, Douglass included a new section about his years living as a fugitive and eventually becoming a free man.

Douglass was alarmed about the 1857 US Supreme Court decision regarding Dred Scott. Dred Scott, a slave, had been taken by his owner to live in a free state, where slavery was against the law. Nonetheless, Scott's owner didn't obey the laws. He kept Scott as his slave and eventually moved back to a slave state. Upon his master's death, ownership of Scott was transferred to his master's widow. Dred Scott argued that he should be a free man because he lived for a time in a free state, but the courts declared otherwise, stating that slaves weren't protected by laws because they were not considered citizens. As a result of this case, Douglass delivered his famous speech, "The Dred Scott Decision," in which he rallied against a government that declared all blacks, slave or free, were not citizens of the United States.

The battle for equality was raging, and Frederick Douglass fought valiantly in the heat of the fray.

The Raid on Harpers Ferry

In late October 1859, a large crowd gathered to hear Frederick Douglass speak at National Hall in Philadelphia. Suddenly, however, a shocking announcement interrupted the meeting. John Brown had attacked a US arsenal at Harpers Ferry, Virginia! Brown's plan had been to steal

Douglass proclaimed to the nation that he could not join in this national holiday celebrating the nation's birth of freedom when millions of Americans still were not free.

Frederick Douglass became active in politics, attending conventions for the Liberty Party where he was chosen for key leadership positions. In 1855 he published his second autobiography,

Harriet Beecher Stowe (1811–1896)

Frederick Douglass recognized the influence Harriet Beecher Stowe's book, *Uncle Tom's Cabin*, had on the abolitionist movement. He stated, "Nothing could have better suited the moral and humane requirements of the hour. Its effect was amazing, instantaneous, and universal. No book on the subject of slavery had so generally and favorably touched the American heart." Before Stowe traveled to England to raise funds to help the cause, she invited Douglass to visit and give his recommendation on how to use the money. Douglass gladly gave his advice and wrote her a letter of endorsement to carry on her trip.

From the collection of the Rochester Public Library Local History Division

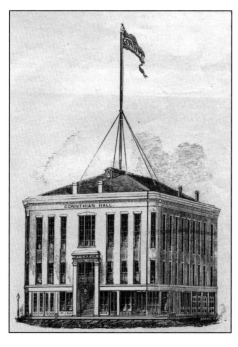

(left) Corinthian Hall, one of Rochester's grandest sites for concerts, balls, lectures, and plays. Frederick Douglass spoke often at this esteemed hall, including his famous speech, "What to the Slave Is the Fourth of July?"
From the collection of the Rochester Public Library Local History Division

(right) Interior view of Corinthian Hall in Rochester, New York.
From the collection of the Rochester Public Library Local History Division

John Brown's raid on
Harpers Ferry.
*Courtesy of the Library of
Congress, LC-USZ62-126970*

the guns at the arsenal and use them to free
slaves.

Frederick Douglass realized immediately that
his friend had finally acted upon his plans. The
next day, more news arrived. Colonel Robert E.
Lee from Virginia and his troops captured John
Brown and his men. Brown's carpetbag was
searched. Letters from Frederick Douglass were
found inside.

"Flee!" urged the friends of Frederick Douglass. But where? How? It was widely known
that Douglass was in Philadelphia. Government
marshals were hot on his trail. Hurried plans
were made to whisk Douglass back to his home
in Rochester in an attempt to outrun the officers
carrying documents for his arrest.

Frederick Douglass quickly dispatched an
anonymous telegram to the telegraph operator in
Rochester, who was a fellow abolitionist:

Tell Lewis (my oldest son) to secure all the
important papers in my high desk.

Any papers from John Brown were hidden.
After a very anxious trip, Frederick Douglass
finally arrived home in Rochester. Minutes later,
there was a knock at his door.

It was a friend along with his neighbor, Lieu-
tenant Governor Selden of New York. Selden
informed Douglass that the governor of New
York undoubtedly would arrest Douglass.

"Leave the country immediately!" his friends
warned.

Frederick Douglass headed for Canada on
the spot. And not a moment too soon. He later
learned that within six hours after he left, US
marshals arrived in Rochester searching for him.

Even though Frederick Douglass had nothing
to do with John Brown's raid, he knew the government would never believe his testimony. Douglass was a friend of Brown's. That alone would
have been enough to sentence Frederick Douglass
to death.

To England and Home Again

After quickly booking a passage to England,
Frederick Douglass braved the cold and choppy

winter sea voyage. Upon reaching Great Britain he said, "England had given me shelter and protection when the slave-hounds were on my track fourteen years before, and her gates were still open to me now that I was pursued in the name of Virginia justice. I could but feel that I was going into exile, perhaps for life."

He spent the next six months in Great Britain lecturing against slavery, speaking about John Brown's raid, and visiting former friends. Suddenly, however, a message reached him. Heart torn with grief, Douglass said, "News reached me from home of the death of my beloved daughter Annie, the light and life of my house. Deeply distressed by this bereavement, and acting upon the impulse of the moment, regardless of the peril, I at once resolved to return home, and took the first outgoing steamer for Portland, Maine."

Douglass returned to his home in Rochester and managed to stay there in secrecy for nearly a month. By this time, however, conditions in America had changed. Political winds had shifted. John Brown was now considered a hero by many, a martyr who sacrificed his life for the freedom of the slave. A great political election took place in the nation. Abraham Lincoln was sworn into office as president of the United States.

An angry South elected its own president. Southern states seceded, or tore away from the Union. The United States was no longer united. Shots were fired. A civil war, great and terrible, was declared.

Frederick Douglass took refuge in England when his life was in danger following John Brown's raid on Harpers Ferry.
Courtesy of the Library of Congress, LC-DIG-cwpbh-05089

~5~

"NOW WE ARE ENGAGED IN A GREAT CIVIL WAR . . ."

A Voice for the Nation

Everywhere he spoke, listeners flocked to hear Frederick Douglass, the famous orator. Frequently lecturing without notes, Douglass listened carefully to other speakers, evaluated the emotions and sentiments of the audience, and then rose to speak out in thunderous tones about the issues at hand.

Frederick Douglass always thought about and spoke about the nation through the eyes of a former slave. He gave his testimony about life as a slave. He urged audiences to consider the slave's point of view and see slavery as the evil it was against human rights. In letters he wrote to political leaders of the day who were also slaveholders, he pressed them to imagine how they would react if their own children were sold into slavery.

Frederick Douglass believed in total equality. He believed in integration in all areas of life, including public transportation,

"Frederick Douglass appealing to President Lincoln and his cabinet" to enlist black troops. Mural by William Edouard Scott at the former Recorder of Deeds building, built in Washington, DC, in 1943. *Courtesy of the Library of Congress, LC-DIG-highsm-09902*

schools, and political and social circles. Wherever he went, often in spite of great resistance, he stepped forward as an equal to everyone else, man or woman, black or white. He saw himself as equal because he believed God made it so.

Deeply religious, Douglass firmly believed that one day God would bring justice and end slavery forever in America. He was a devout Christian, yet Douglass was also outspoken against the "Christianity" of the slaveholders. He argued that no one could be called a Christian who owned another person, even if that slave was treated with kindness. The sheer act of owning another human being, Douglass declared, was against the biblical principles of God.

Frederick Douglass believed one person could make a difference. He took it upon himself to integrate public education in Rochester, and he succeeded. He took it upon himself to integrate public transportation wherever he went, and he succeeded. Through the papers he published, the speeches he gave, and the actions he took, Douglass took it upon himself to help bring an end to slavery, and he succeeded. He dedicated his life to freeing the slave and establishing equal rights.

Frederick Douglass had one of the most brilliant minds this world has known. And when he heard that the first shots of the Civil War had been fired, he hurried to his newspaper office and printed an article stating, "God be praised! that it has come at last."

A Great Visionary

As an American, Frederick Douglass was not thankful for the war. Yet looking at the situation through the eyes of a former slave, Douglass was deeply thankful that the time had come to break the chains of slavery. His heart united with the hearts of every slave and fugitive upon hearing the news that the Civil War had begun. Freedom! At long last, the slaves would be free!

A true visionary, Frederick Douglass immediately rose up and rallied a two-fold cry. Just one month after the beginning of the war, he published two points in an article in his newspaper, "How to End the War."

Over 10,000 African Americans served in the Union Navy.
Courtesy of the Library of Congress, LC-DIG-ppmsca-36959

"Freedom to the slave should now be proclaimed from the Capitol," Frederick Douglass cried, "and should be seen above the smoke and fire of every battle field, waving from every loyal flag!" Douglass believed the first thing to do to bring an end to the war was to immediately emancipate, or set free, every slave.

The second thing Douglass believed would end the war quickly was to enlist black troops. He declared, "We have no hesitation in saying that ten thousand black soldiers might be raised in the next thirty days to march upon the South. One black regiment alone would be, in such a war, the full equal of two white ones."

Frederick Douglass lectured about this all over the northern states. He wrote urgent letters to political leaders, repeating the message. He traveled to Washington, DC, and shared his message with President Lincoln. He believed he knew the way to end the war, and he was right. It just took the rest of the nation, its political leaders, and its president several dreadful and devastating years to realize what Frederick Douglass had known from the beginning. The Civil War was a war about slavery, and the only way to bring it to an end was to free the slaves and allow black soldiers to fight.

The Douglass' Monthly

Frederick Douglass renamed his newspaper the *Douglass' Monthly*. During the war, he championed the cry to free the slaves and enlist black troops. Eager to see the war quickly brought to

Born a slave, Sergeant Milton M. Holland later received his freedom, perhaps because he appeared white. When war was declared, he joined the private militia, Attucks Guards, before recruiting for and enlisting in the 5th US Colored Troops (USCT). He received the Medal of Honor for his heroism during battle.
Courtesy of the Library of Congress, LC-USZ62-118552

an end, the *Douglass' Monthly* became a platform for other abolitionists to join his crusade.

In the *Douglass' Monthly*, Frederick Douglass followed the progress the nation was making toward emancipation and enlistment of black troops. In the numerous articles he wrote, he pressured Lincoln to move forward on both agendas. He also urged the people of the Union to join his cause. "From the first," Douglass admitted, "I reproached the North that they fought the rebels with only one hand, when they might strike effectually with two—that they fought with their soft white hand, while they kept their black iron hand chained and helpless behind them."

His war effort was not limited to his newspaper's readership, however. Frederick Douglass stated, "In every way possible—in the columns of my paper and on the platform, by letters to friends, at home and abroad, I did all that I could to improve this conviction upon the country."

Disappointed with the nation's decision not to enlist black troops, Frederick Douglass rejoiced with each step the Union took toward emancipation and arming black regiments. When General Butler announced the policy to receive runaway slaves as "contrabands" of war who could enjoy freedom within Union lines, Douglass was vocal in his approval.

Frederick Douglass was well aware of how the South already employed slaves to supply the Confederate army. The slave, Douglass explained, "was not only the stomach of the rebellion, by supplying its commissary department, but he built its forts, dug its entrenchments, and performed other duties of the camp which left the rebel soldier more free to fight the loyal army than he could otherwise have been."

Douglass approved of Lincoln's policy to enlist 50,000 African Americans for building fortifications, scouting, and foraging. "At last, the truth began to dawn up on the administration that the Negro might be made useful to loyalty, as well as to treason, to the Union as well as to the Confederacy," Douglass said. And with this small step forward, Frederick Douglass stepped up the pressure to lobby Lincoln to free all slaves and raise troops of African American soldiers.

The Summer of Change

Both sides of the Civil War experienced horrible and devastating losses on battlefields. But now the Union army had a new problem. Everywhere they marched deeper and deeper into the South, African Americans escaped and joined Union lines, many bringing along their entire families. Others joined the tide to search for family members who had been sold.

Harriet Tubman (1820-1913)

Almost single-handedly, Harriet Tubman journeyed deep into southern territory, organized small groups of escaping slaves, and personally led them to freedom in the North. After the Civil War broke out, she served the Union as a spy, nurse, and army scout. (Note the haversack she is carrying.) Friend and fellow abolitionist Frederick Douglass gladly wrote an endorsement for her biography, *Scenes in the Life of Harriet Tubman.*

From the collection of the Rochester Public Library Local History Division

The Native Guards

Also known as the Corps d'Afrique, the 1st Regiment Louisiana Native Guards (many of them free wealthy landowners) organized to protect their lands in rebel territory. When Union forces overtook New Orleans, the Native Guards joined the Union and fought bravely in major battles of the war. The regiment's famous captain, André Cailloux, and its line officers were African American. Many of these soldiers had ancestors who fought in the War of 1812.

Native Guards attack the Confederate defensive at Port Hudson.
Courtesy of the Library of Congress, LC-USZ62-133081

Frederick Douglass had a solution to this problem: free the slave and enlist him to fight! Various Union generals agreed.

When Union troops took over the South Carolina Sea Islands, white plantation owners ran off, leaving thousands of slaves behind. Evaluating the situation, General Hunter announced freedom for all slaves who joined his Union troops. Frederick Douglass heartily supported this policy. "Many and grievous disasters on flood and field were needed to educate the loyal nation and President Lincoln up to the realization of the necessity, not to say justice, of this position, and many devices, intermediate steps, and make-shifts were suggested to smooth the way to the ultimate policy of freeing the slave, and arming the freedman."

> **"The arm of the slave was the best defense against the arm of the slaveholder." —Frederick Douglass**

Even President Lincoln began to see the practicality and necessity of offering freedom to the slaves. Not only would this cut the Confederate army's labor force, but it would provide much-needed laborers for the Union army and, as Lincoln finally conceded, much-needed troops.

In September 1862 President Lincoln declared he would issue the Emancipation Proclamation on the upcoming New Year's Day. Frederick Douglass and fellow abolitionists rejoiced. Plans were made to celebrate the joyous news.

CARRY A CIVIL WAR HAVERSACK

During the Civil War, soldiers were issued a haversack, or type of bag, to carry their rations in. The haversack could hold about three days of rations, or food supplies. The Union gave each soldier a waterproof haversack made of tar-covered canvas as part of his uniform. Soldiers in the Confederate army usually had to make their own and sewed theirs from heavy fabric.

If you want your haversack to appear waterproof, paint the finished haversack with black glossy acrylic fabric paint.

Materials

* ½ yard white cotton duck fabric
* Ruler
* Fabric scissors
* Pencil
* Safety pins or straight pins
* White thread
* Sewing machine
* Black glossy acrylic fabric paint and paint supplies (optional)

Adult supervision required

➡ Cut a 14 x 33-inch rectangle from the heavy fabric for the body of the haversack. Then cut a 5 x 44-inch strip to form the strap.

To form the flap on the haversack, measure down the long side 7 inches from one corner and draw a dot. Measure and draw a matching dot on the opposite side. Across the top, measure to the middle (7 inches) and draw a dot. Fold the fabric over to the middle from both corners to form the flap (from dot to dot) and pin it in place. Sew along the fold, ½ inch from the edge of the flap. Trim off the excess fabric.

Along the bottom 14-inch edge, fold up 1 inch of fabric and sew along the fold, ½ inch from the edge.

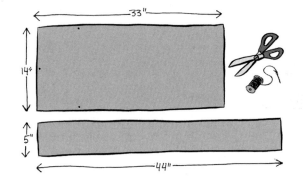

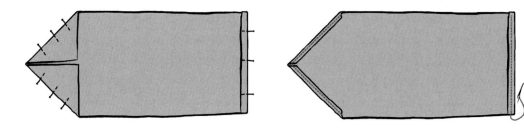

To form the strap, fold over ½ inch from both edges of the long sides, pinning in place. Then fold the piece in half with the raw edges inside. Stitch the entire length of the strap, close to the folded edges.

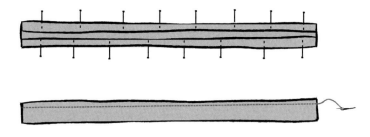

Lay the body of the haversack on a table with the unfinished edges underneath (right side facing up). Position one end of the strap 1 inch below the dot on the right side. Position the other end of the strap 1 inch below the dot on the left side. Check that the strap is not twisted but will lie flat when done.

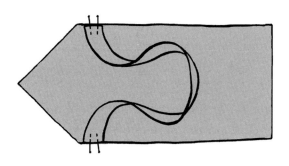

Fold up the bottom of the haversack, right sides together, and sandwich the edges of the straps in between the front and back layers. Stitch up both sides of the haversack, going back and forth over the top edge to reinforce the opening.

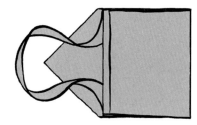 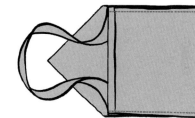

Turn the haversack right side out. Fold over the flap to close it. Wear the haversack over your shoulder so it won't fall off while you're walking.

Susie King Taylor (1842–1912)

A nurse and laundress for the 1st South Carolina Volunteers (later to become known as the 33rd USCT), Susie King Taylor wrote an autobiography about her experiences, *Reminiscences of My Life in Camp*. Taylor's husband served in the Union army. Along with her duties caring for the wounded and sick, Susie King Taylor also taught many soldiers to read.

Courtesy of Documenting the American South, the University of North Carolina at Chapel Hill Libraries

A Grand and Glorious Celebration

On New Year's Day, 1863, Frederick Douglass was in Boston. A large crowd gathered throughout the entire day at Tremont Temple to await the news. Another crowd of similar size gathered nearby at Music Hall. Would President Lincoln actually issue the Emancipation Proclamation?

Douglass hurried through the cold, chilly air to join fellow abolitionists at Tremont Temple. Once there, he found William C. Nell, William Wells Brown, and other friends. Short speeches were made, including those by Brown and Douglass. Nobody felt like speaking, however. All were eager for news from the White House.

The clock ticked on into the evening. Darkness fell. Eight o'clock. Nine o'clock. Douglass took a deep breath. He worried. "Every moment of waiting chilled our hopes, and strengthened our fears," he admitted. And still the clock ticked on with no word from Washington. Ten o'clock came and went. The evening soon would be over. Douglass wrestled with feelings of agony. Would Lincoln be true to his word? Would he actually emancipate the slaves? "We were waiting and listening as for a bolt from the sky, which should rend the fetters of four millions of slaves; we were watching, as it were, by the dim light of the stars, for the dawn of a new day; we were longing for the answer to the agonizing prayers of centuries."

Suddenly a man pushed his way through the crowd. Time froze. Douglass never forgot the moment. "With a face fairly illumined with the news he bore," Douglass shared, he "exclaimed in tones that thrilled all hearts, 'It is coming! It is on the wires!!'"

Shouts of joy filled the air. Men and women, black and white, broke down in sobs, tears shining on their glad faces. Douglass and his friends rejoiced. The celebration was so exuberant that no one was ready to leave by midnight when the hall closed. The celebration moved down the street to continue at Twelfth Baptist Church, the largest black church in Boston. As the new day dawned, the voices of the multitude rang out with joy. "It was one of the most affecting and thrilling occasions I ever witnessed," Frederick Douglass rejoiced. The slave was now free!

> **"The first of January, 1863, was a memorable day in the progress of American liberty and civilization. It was the turning-point in the conflict between freedom and slavery." —Frederick Douglass**

Celebrations took place all over the North and wherever Union troops were stationed in the South. In her diary, Charlotte Forten (Grimké) wrote about the festivities that took place near Beaufort, South Carolina, where she volunteered as a teacher to the newly freed slaves on the South Carolina Sea Islands. Forten described New Year's Day 1863 as "the most glorious day this nation as yet seen." She observed with great pride the black soldiers ready to defend the Union and joined in singing the "John Brown Song." At the end of this special ceremony, African Americans in the crowd, most of them recently freed from slavery, spontaneously burst forth singing, "My Country 'Tis of Thee." Everyone was moved deeply at the significance of this moment.

Recruit!

With the authorization to raise African American regiments, Frederick Douglass took a position with the government as a recruiting agent. He

The 1st South Carolina Volunteers receive the Stars and Stripes at the Emancipation Day celebration on Smith's plantation, Port Royal, South Carolina. *Courtesy of the Library of Congress, LC-USZ62-88808*

Charlotte Forten (Grimké) (1837-1914)

Born into a wealthy family of free blacks from Philadelphia, Charlotte Forten was the granddaughter of famous abolitionist, inventor, and businessman James Forten, beloved niece of Robert Purvis, and cousin of leading physician Charles Burleigh Purvis. As a young woman, she traveled to the South Carolina Sea Islands during the Civil War where she volunteered to teach newly freed slaves. Her diary of this experience reveals a unique perspective of the war. Years later, she and her husband, Francis J. Grimké, were friends with Frederick Douglass and his family.

Courtesy of Moorland-Spingarn Research Center, Howard University

"JOHN BROWN SONG"

➡ The "John Brown Song" was one of the Union's favorite songs. Wherever they marched, black troops could be heard jubilantly singing the tune. When Charleston fell, the Massachusetts 54th and 55th were the first Union troops to march into the city and entered singing the "John Brown Song." Soldiers often added lyrics to the tune, a familiar hymn of the day. Julia Ward Howe wrote new words to accompany the melody, which became the "Battle Hymn of the Republic."

To hear one version of this famous song, visit the Library of Congress website at http://lcweb2.loc.gov/diglib/ihas/loc.natlib. ihas.100010565/default.html. On the left of the page, click on the link to listen to one of the Audio Formats on your computer.

Now it's your turn to sing this song.

John Brown's body lies a mouldering in the grave.
(Sing three times.)
His soul's marching on!

Chorus:
Glory Hally, Hallelujah! *(Sing three times.)*
His soul's marching on!

He's gone to be a soldier in the army of our Lord.
(Sing three times.)
His soul's marching on!
Chorus

John Brown's knapsack is strapped upon his back.
(Sing three times.)
His soul's marching on!
Chorus

His pet lambs will meet him on the way. *(Sing three times.)*
They go marching on!
Chorus

Now, three rousing cheers for the Union! *(Sing three times.)*
As we are marching on!
Chorus
Hip, hip, hip, hip Hurrah!

Try writing new verses to tell about the brave soldiers who fought to bring an end to slavery. Or sing about the men and women who worked behind the battle lines, such as Frederick Douglass and Harriet Tubman. Write down your lyrics and share the song with your friends.

traveled throughout the northern states signing up recruitments for the Massachusetts 54th and 55th Volunteers. His two sons, Charles and Lewis, were the first men to enlist from the state of New York.

Other recruiting agents included Douglass's friends Martin R. Delany, William Wells Brown, and Mary Ann Shadd Cary. Delany, who had worked with Douglass years before to publish the *North Star*, had a son in the Massachusetts 54th as well. Toussaint L'Ouverture Delany and Lewis Douglass both fought valiantly in the heroic assault on Fort Wagner—and lived to tell about it.

Frederick Douglass's pride in all the black soldiers was immense. "The 54th was not long in the field," Douglass said, "before it proved itself gallant and strong, worthy to rank with the most courageous of its white companions in arms. Its assault upon Fort Wagner, in which it was so fearfully cut to pieces, and lost nearly half its officers, including its beloved and trusted commander, Col. Shaw, at once gave it a name and a fame throughout the country. In that terrible battle, under the wing of night, more cavils in respect of the quality of Negro manhood were set at rest than could have been during a century of ordinary life and observation."

When Sergeant Major Lewis Douglass fought in the assault on Fort Wagner, he reached the parapet and shouted, "Come, boys, come, let's fight for God and Governor Andrew!" As retreat became essential, Douglass was the last to leave the parapet to return to safety.

Sergeant William Carney seized the flag and carried it bravely through the assault on Fort Wagner in spite of serious wounds. He received the Medal of Honor for his heroism.
Courtesy of the Library of Congress, LC-USZ62-118558

Mary Ann Shadd Cary (1823–1893)

Born into a family of abolitionists, Mary Ann Shadd Cary carried the antislavery torch into the next generation. After the Fugitive Slave Act of 1850 was passed, she relocated to Canada, where she helped publish the antislavery newspaper the *Provincial Freeman* before moving back to the United States. Along with Frederick Douglass, Mary Ann Shadd Cary helped recruit black troops during the Civil War.

Image Courtesy of Documenting the American South, the University of North Carolina at Chapel Hill Libraries

CIVIL WAR TIME LINE

∽ 1861 ∽

April • Confederacy attacks Fort Sumter.

May • Frederick Douglass rallies two-fold cry: "Immediate emancipation and enlist black troops!"

Spring • Confederacy uses slaves for noncombat duties.
- African American leaders in New York offer to organize and finance black regiments.
- African American leaders in Philadelphia form two black regiments.
- Jacob Dodson and 300 free blacks volunteer in Washington, DC. Similar offers pour in from free blacks across the North.
- Offers to raise black troops are denied by the government.

July • After the cargo ship *S. J. Waring* is captured by Confederates, navy hero William Tillman takes over and sails the ship back to Union lines.

Summer • African Americans serve the Union in noncombat duties.
- Union Navy enlists free blacks as cooks and assistant gunners.
- Frederick Douglass pressures Lincoln to emancipate all slaves and enlist black troops.

August • General Frémont in Missouri issues statement that all slaves joining the Union army will be declared free. Lincoln opposes the statement.

Fall • At Fort Monroe, Virginia, General Butler announces that slaves escaping to Union lines are "contrabands of war" and won't be returned to owners.
- Slaves escape to Fort Monroe. Contraband camps form wherever Union troops advance.

Union soldier from Company B, 103rd Regiment, wearing forage cap.
Courtesy of the Library of Congress, LC-ppmsca-26988

∽ 1862 ∽

April • Union army takes New Orleans. Native Guard, the elite regiment of free blacks, offers to fight. By November, three infantry regiments and one regiment of heavy artillery are organized, including 75 African American officers.

Spring • Robert Smalls kidnaps the Confederate steamboat *Planter* and pilots her to Union forces.

Robert Smalls and the gunboat Planter.
Courtesy of the Library of Congress, LC-USZ62-89569

- General Hunter declares all slaves free who join his troops in the South Carolina Sea Islands.
- Union Navy enlists contrabands to serve in all roles.
- Massachusetts governor sends Harriet Tubman to Hilton Head, South Carolina, as a nurse. Tubman leads a spy network from South Carolina to Florida.
- General Hunter organizes the First South Carolina Volunteers.

Summer • Susie King Taylor joins the First South Carolina Volunteers as a nurse and laundress, remaining until the end of the war.
- Confederacy passes law to kill black Union soldiers or their white officers if captured.

October
- Black regiment First Kansas Volunteers organizes.
- First Kansas Volunteers engage in battle near Butler, Missouri.

Guarding the cannon at City Point, Virginia.
Courtesy of the Library of Congress, LC-DIG-cwpb-01982

~ 1863 ~

January 1
- President Lincoln issues the Emancipation Proclamation.
- Frederick Douglass and other abolitionists celebrate.

Winter
- Lincoln authorizes raising two black regiments in Massachusetts.
- Frederick Douglass publishes his famous "Men of Color, to Arms!" and fellow abolitionists join him to recruit black troops.

Charles Douglass, son of Frederick Douglass.
Courtesy of Moorland-Spingarn Research Center, Howard University

- Lewis and Charles Douglass, sons of Frederick Douglass, join the 54th Massachusetts Volunteers.

March
- South Carolina Volunteers take Jacksonville, Florida.

April
- Lewis Douglass is appointed Sergeant Major of the 54th Massachusetts Volunteers.

May
- War Department authorizes the United States Colored Troops (USCT), segregated black troops led by white officers.
- Native Guard storms Port Hudson, allowing Union forces to overtake the fort.

July
- Massachusetts 54th leads charge on Fort Wagner. Sergeant William Carney is the first of over 20 African Americans to earn the Medal of Honor.
- Frederick Douglass visits President Lincoln to pressure government for equal rights for black troops.

Picket station at Dutch Gap, Virginia.
Courtesy of the Library of Congress, LC-DIG-cwpb-01930

Summer
- Frederick Douglass Jr. recruits black troops in Mississippi.

August
- After 15 years as editor of his newspapers, Frederick Douglass ends publication of the *Douglass' Monthly* to devote more efforts to recruitment.

Fall
- Alexander T. Augusta is commissioned as surgeon for the 7th USCT.

September
- USCT troops protest unequal wages, refusing to accept any pay until it is equal pay. Many of their white officers join the protest.

continued . . .

African American soldiers.
Courtesy of the Library of Congress, LC-USZ62-105556

CIVIL WAR TIME LINE continued . . .

~ 1864 ~

February • In heavy fighting at Olustee, Florida, the 54th Massachusetts and other black troops distinguish themselves for bravery.

April • Fort Pillow massacre of black troops in Tennessee.

July • Black troops suffer tragic losses in a battle at Petersburg, Virginia, known as "The Crater."

August • Lincoln invites Douglass to visit and give advice.

Sergeant Major Christian Fleetwood.
Courtesy of the Library of Congress,
LC-USZ62-118565

• Sergeant Major Christian Fleetwood, 4th Regiment USCT, earns a Medal of Honor in the battle of New Market Heights.

• General Sherman's March to the Sea begins. Contrabands pour into Union lines and help make the campaign successful.

Fall • USCT help win major battles everywhere they fight.

~ 1865 ~

February • Charleston, Virginia, falls. The Massachusetts 54th and 55th are among the first Union troops to enter the city.

• Martin R. Delany is commissioned as a major in the US Army.

Spring • Congress approves equal pay for USCT, including back pay from the date of enlistment.

Sergeant Major Thomas R. Hawkins, Medal of Honor recipient.
Courtesy of the Library of Congress,
LC-USZ62-118559

April • Petersburg falls. Black troops are the first to march into the city, singing "John Brown Song." Remaining black troops join Ulysses S. Grant to chase Confederate troops.

April • Richmond, Virginia, falls and the USCT Cavalry leads Union troops as they ride in to take over the city.

• Black war correspondent Thomas Morris Chester covers the fall of Richmond and other news from the front for the major daily newspaper the *Philadelphia Press*.

• Lee surrenders to Grant at Appomattox on April 9.

• Robert Smalls pilots the *Planter* with African American passengers to join the celebration after Union troops take over Fort Sumter.

• Union cavalry advances through North Carolina and well-known poet George Moses Horton is finally set free.

June 19 • Union troops ride into Galveston, Texas, and officially free the last group of slaves (still held in captivity even after war's end). Juneteenth is celebrated each year to commemorate this historic event.

Sergeant John Lawson stayed at his station through the heat of the battle on the deck of the warship *Hartford*.
Courtesy of the Library of Congress,
LC-USZ62-118553

A Letter Home

Frederick Douglass's son Lewis Douglass wrote home to tell his sweetheart of the terrible battle he fought when his troop led the assault on Fort Wagner.

MORRIS ISLAND. S. C. July 20

MY DEAR AMELIA:

I have been in two fights, and am unhurt. I am about to go in another I believe to-night. Our men fought well on both occasions. The last was desperate we charged that terrible battery on Morris Island known as Fort Wagoner, and were repulsed with a loss of 3 killed and wounded. I escaped unhurt from amidst that perfect hail of shot and shell. It was terrible. I need not particularize the papers will give a better than I have time to give. My thoughts are with you often, you are as dear as ever, be good enough to remember it as I no doubt you will. As I said before we are on the eve of another fight and I am very busy and have just snatched a moment to write you. I must necessarily be brief. Should I fall in the next fight killed or wounded I hope to fall with my face to the foe.

If I survive I shall write you a long letter. DeForrest of your city is wounded George Washington is missing, Jacob Carter is missing, Chas Reason wounded Chas Whiting, Chas Creamer all wounded. The above are in hospital.

This regiment has established its reputation as a fighting regiment not a man flinched, though it was a trying time. Men fell all around me. A shell would explode and clear a space of twenty feet, our men would close up again, but it was no use we had to retreat, which was a very hazardous undertaking. How I got out of that fight alive I cannot tell, but I am here. My Dear girl I hope again to see you. I must bid you farewell should I be killed. Remember if I die I die in a good cause. I wish we had a hundred thousand colored troops we would put an end to this war.

Good Bye to all Write soon
Your own loving LEWIS

Two Great Men

Frederick Douglass met with President Abraham Lincoln twice at the White House during the Civil War. For his first visit, Douglass felt compelled to go. "My efforts to secure just and fair treatment for the colored soldiers did not stop at letters and speeches," Douglass explained. "I was induced to go to Washington and lay the complaints of my people before President Lincoln."

Although he was a famous abolitionist and brilliant orator, Douglass felt unsure about meeting with the president but nonetheless felt it extremely urgent. "I need not say that at the time I undertook this mission it required much more nerve than a similar one would require now," Douglass remembered. "The distance between

Lewis Douglass, son of Frederick Douglass. *Courtesy of Moorland-Spingarn Research Center, Howard University*

Frederick Douglass visited President Lincoln at the White House in Washington, DC.
Photo by author

The room bore the marks of business, and the persons in it, the president included, appeared to be much overworked and tired. Long lines of care were already deeply written on Mr. Lincoln's brow, and his strong face, full of earnestness, lighted up as soon as my name was mentioned. As I approached and was introduced to him he arose and extended his hand, and bade me welcome. I at once felt myself in the presence of an honest man—one whom I could love, honor, and trust without reserve or doubt. Proceeding to tell him who I was and what I was doing, he promptly, but kindly, stopped me, saying: "I know who you are, Mr. Douglass."

The president invited Douglass to sit down. Frederick Douglass explained the reason for his visit, "that the government did not, in several respects, deal fairly" with the black soldiers fighting on behalf of the Union. President Lincoln asked Douglass to give him details.

Douglass outlined three major points. First, he stated that black troops should receive the same pay as white soldiers. Second, black soldiers should receive the same protection when captured as white soldiers did. And finally, black soldiers should receive the same awards for heroism on the battlefield.

President Lincoln discussed all three issues openly with Douglass. When Frederick Douglass left the White House, he concluded, "Though I was not entirely satisfied with his views, I was so

the black man and the white American citizen was immeasurable. I was an ex-slave, identified with a despised race, and yet I was to meet the most exalted person in this great republic. It was altogether an unwelcome duty, and one from which I would gladly have been excused. I could not know what kind of a reception would be accorded me."

The meeting of these two great men, Frederick Douglass and Abraham Lincoln, stands as a landmark in the shifting sands of time. "I shall never forget my first interview with this great man," Frederick Douglass said. He was shown into the room where the president received visitors.

Sojourner Truth (1797-1883)

As a famous abolitionist and outspoken advocate of women's rights, Sojourner Truth traveled extensively to promote civil rights. A former slave, she shared the speaker's platform at various times with Frederick Douglass. During the Civil War, Sojourner Truth visited with President Lincoln.

Courtesy of the Library of Congress, LC-USZ62-16225

First Sergeant Powhatan Beaty received the Medal of Honor for taking command of his unit in a fierce battle after all the white officers had been killed.
Courtesy of the Library of Congress, LC-USZ62-118556

well satisfied with the man and with the educating tendency of the conflict that I determined to go on with the recruiting."

At the time, Douglass didn't know whether his visit had made any difference. But it had. By the end of the war, black troops were receiving equal pay, retroactive to the time of their enlistment. Laws were made to give them better protection. And over 20 African Americans were awarded the Medal of Honor for heroism during battle.

An Invitation

The second time Frederick Douglass met with Abraham Lincoln was in response to an invitation the president sent to him to ask for advice.

President Lincoln openly discussed his fears that the Civil War might end and slavery not end with it. "What he said on this day showed a deeper moral conviction against slavery than I had ever seen before in anything spoken or written by him," Douglass said.

The president expressed his dismay that not as many slaves were joining Union forces as he had hoped after he issued the Emancipation Proclamation. Douglass explained to him that "slaveholders knew how to keep such things from their slaves, and probably very few knew of his proclamation." They discussed plans for Douglass to raise a band of spies and scouts who could sneak deep into the South and declare emancipation to slaves, urging them to escape and join Union troops.

While Douglass talked with the president, another visitor was announced who wished to speak with Lincoln. "Tell Governor Buckingham to wait, for I want to have a long talk with my friend Frederick Douglass," was President Lincoln's reply. Douglass insisted he could wait while the other visitor was attended to, but Lincoln would not hear of it.

This demonstration of respect touched Douglass deeply. Even though Douglass often disagreed strongly with Lincoln's politics—for example, Lincoln's viewpoints on issues such as colonization (Lincoln supported having free blacks move away from America, which Douglass strongly opposed) or immediate equal rights for black troops—he also held a great measure of respect for the president. "I have often said elsewhere," Douglass stated, "what I wish to repeat here, that Mr. Lincoln was not only a great president, but a *great man*—too great to be small in anything."

Frederick Douglass left the White House with intentions to fulfill the president's plans. But the winds of war rapidly changed. Shortly after this meeting, President Lincoln received news that Union troops had taken over Atlanta, Georgia. William Tecumseh Sherman's March to the Sea would begin. This great victory would bring the support the president needed for reelection and help bring a final end to slavery.

CREATE A MEMORY

➡ Honoring African American heroes who served during the Civil War, the African American Civil War Memorial and Museum opened its doors in 2011, 150 years after the first shots were fired at Fort Sumter. The museum is collecting information, artifacts, photographs, letters, and stories from families whose relatives were enlisted in the USCT.

You can help our nation create a lasting memory. Search through photo albums, old letters, and souvenirs in your family's treasured collections. Visit your grandparents, aunts, or uncles, and ask the oldest ones to tell you stories about the Civil War that their ancestors told them. If you have a relative who enlisted in the USCT, the segregated black troops led by white officers, search for his name at the National Park Service Civil War Soldiers and Sailors index at www.itd.nps.gov/cwss/soldiers.cfm.

Write down the information you find. Take videos of your relatives talking about the stories they remember. Write some of their stories down. Then get in touch with the African American Civil War Memorial and Museum by looking up the contact information on their website at www.afroamcivilwar.org. Share your discoveries with the museum.

The Question of Civil Rights

By the middle of the Civil War, Frederick Douglass rallied a new cry. Douglass urged his audiences to consider the freedom and civil rights of newly freed slaves. Having grown up within the slave system Douglass understood, as few other leaders in the North could, that simply winning a war could not change attitudes of hatred, violence, and oppression that had ruled in the rebel states for generations.

The great visionary that he was, Frederick Douglass predicted that the rights of former slaves would quickly be overthrown unless drastic actions were taken. He urged antislavery societies to continue their work, changing their focus from bringing an end to slavery to bringing freedoms and civil rights to the former slave. This became his new passion, his new life work, and his new focus. It would continue after the war came to an end and all his predictions came true.

An End and a New Beginning

The Civil War, great and terrible, finally came to an end. Frederick Douglass rejoiced along with the nation, sad and tired as it was from four years of devastation and loss. Plans began to take shape for restoring the war-torn nation.

(left) Frederick Douglass spoke at Faneuil Hall in Boston to celebrate the news of the fall of Richmond, the capital of the Confederacy. *Photo by author*

(right) When famous orator Frederick Douglass spoke to a packed audience here inside Faneuil Hall to celebrate the fall of Richmond, he shared the speaker's platform with Robert Winthrop. This was the same aristocrat Douglass had once served 25 years earlier as a waiter in the mansion of the upcoming governor of Massachusetts. *Photo by author*

"After the fall of Richmond the collapse of the rebellion was not long delayed," Douglass said, "though it did not perish without adding to its long list of atrocities one which sent a thrill of horror throughout the civilized world, in the assassination of Abraham Lincoln."

Douglass remembers that he was at his home in Rochester, New York, when news of the president's murder came speeding along the wires. "Our citizens," Douglass said, "not knowing what else to do in the agony of the hour, betook themselves to the city hall. Though all hearts ached for utterance, few felt like speaking. We were stunned and overwhelmed by a crime and calamity hitherto unknown to our country and to our government."

Near the end of the gathering, Douglass was called upon to speak. He rose and spoke from a heart filled with grief.

After that night, Douglass returned home and reflected on his life, the end of the Civil War, the end of slavery, and now Lincoln's assassination. Douglass had dedicated his life to bringing an end to slavery in America. He shared, "My great and exceeding joy over these stupendous achievements, especially over the abolition of slavery (which had been the deepest desire and the great labor of my life), was slightly tinged with a feeling of sadness."

His life's great work was behind him. What future could lie ahead?

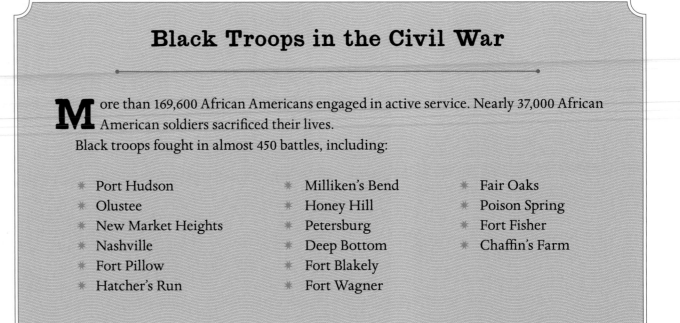

Black Troops in the Civil War

More than 169,600 African Americans engaged in active service. Nearly 37,000 African American soldiers sacrificed their lives.

Black troops fought in almost 450 battles, including:

* Port Hudson
* Olustee
* New Market Heights
* Nashville
* Fort Pillow
* Hatcher's Run

* Milliken's Bend
* Honey Hill
* Petersburg
* Deep Bottom
* Fort Blakely
* Fort Wagner

* Fair Oaks
* Poison Spring
* Fort Fisher
* Chaffin's Farm

The Colored Soldiers

BY PAUL LAURENCE DUNBAR *(selected stanzas)*

"The 54th Massachusetts regiment, under the leadership of Colonel Shaw in the attack on Fort Wagner, Morris Island, South Carolina, in 1863." Mural at the former Recorder of Deeds building built in Washington, DC, in 1943. *Courtesy of the Library of Congress, LC-DIG-highsm-09903*

If the muse were mine to tempt it
And my feeble voice were strong,
If my tongue were trained to measures,
I would sing a stirring song.
I would sing a song heroic
Of those noble sons of Ham,*
Of the gallant colored soldiers
Who fought for Uncle Sam!**

Ah, they rallied to the standard***
To uphold it by their might;
None were stronger in the labors,
None were braver in the fight.
From the blazing breach of Wagner
To the plains of Olustee,
They were foremost in the fight
Of the battles of the free.

And their deeds shall find a record
In the registry of Fame;
For their blood has cleansed completely
Every blot of Slavery's shame.
So all honor and all glory
To those noble sons of Ham—
The gallant colored soldiers
Who fought for Uncle Sam!

Ham was a son of Noah from the Bible who is said to be an ancestor of the African race.
**Uncle Sam is a common nickname for the United States.*
***The standard is the American flag.*

~ 6 ~

"THAT THIS NATION, UNDER GOD, SHALL HAVE A NEW BIRTH OF FREEDOM . . ."

The Nation's New Hour

The Civil War was over. With the last cannon blast fired on the battlefield came the last shriek of a mother's breaking heart as she stood on the slave's auction block and her children were stolen from her arms. Slavery in America had come to an end.

The joy Frederick Douglass felt in his heart was indescribable. He had dedicated his life's work to bringing an end to slavery. In his highest hopes, however, he had never dared to imagine what life would be like if slavery actually ended. Yet it had. He had lived to see the end of slavery in his own lifetime.

Now he felt at a loss. He said, "I felt that I had reached the end of the noblest and best part of my life; my school was broken up, my church disbanded, and the beloved congregation

Commissioners to Santo Domingo. (Frederick Douglass, far left.)
Courtesy of Documenting the American South, the University of North Carolina at Chapel Hill Libraries

dispersed, never to come together again. The antislavery platform had performed its work, and my voice was no longer needed."

What should he do next? The antislavery societies had dissolved, and he no longer had a job. What employment could he find to support his family? He was about 48 years old. His children were now grown and could support themselves, but he and Anna still had their life before them.

Frederick Douglass considered purchasing a small farm and living off the land. He had not considered, however, the fact that his country needed him. War-torn, tired, and suffering from its grievous losses, America needed Frederick Douglass to help bring healing to the new nation.

"Invitations began to pour in upon me," Douglass said, "from colleges, lyceums, and literary societies." People yearned to hear the voice of inspiration that only Frederick Douglass could deliver. Often they requested his well-known speech, "Self-Made Men." Offers flooded in to pay him $100 or $200 to appear for a single lecture. What a huge difference this was in comparison to the $450 he previously made in an entire year while lecturing for the American Antislavery Society!

The Power of the Ballot

As the year unfolded following the surrender at Appomattox, it soon became obvious that even though slavery was no longer a legal institution, the newfound rights of the freed slaves were violently being torn from their grasp. What

Frederick Douglass had predicted since the middle of the war was now happening. Former slaveholders developed new methods of keeping the freedmen in bondage.

> "Though they were not slaves, they were not yet quite free. No man can be truly free whose liberty is dependent upon the thought, feeling, and action of others, and who has himself no means in his own hands for guarding, protecting, defending, and maintaining that liberty."
> —Frederick Douglass

Frederick Douglass discovered his new life's work. He explained, "I therefore soon found that the Negro had still a cause, and that he needed my voice and pen with others to plead for it." Douglass traveled throughout the states, urging the absolute necessity of giving power to the black man by giving him the right to vote.

Together with a delegation made up of his son Lewis, his friends, and his fellow leaders, Frederick Douglass met with President Andrew Johnson to discuss the necessity of giving black men the power to vote.

After this historic meeting, Douglass and his associates drafted a letter and submitted it to the US Senate, once again urging the necessity of giving black men the vote. Enfranchisement, or

MAKE A CANE

After Abraham Lincoln's assassination, his widow, Mary Todd Lincoln, gave Frederick Douglass this walking stick that belonged to the president in honor of Douglass's efforts to help end slavery.

Materials

* Straight tree branch or wooden dowel rod that is 1 inch thick and 36 inches long (Note: If you will be attaching a cane tip or handle to your cane, be sure to choose a thickness of wood that will fit the accessories.)
* Pocketknife (optional)
* Sandpaper
* Pencil
* Wood-burning tool (optional)
* Permanent marker
* Cane tip or handle (optional)

Adult supervision required

➥ If you are using a branch, ask an adult to help you strip the bark from the branch using a pocketknife. Sand the wood with sandpaper until it is smooth. Use a pencil to draw a design on the wood. When you are satisfied with the design, make it permanent by either whittling with a pocketknife (with an adult's permission), charring the wood with a wood-burning tool, or tracing over the penciled design with a permanent marker. When you are finished, attach a cane tip to the bottom or a handle to the top of the wood piece if you want. Cane tips and handles are available at online stores such as Treeline (www.treelineusa.com) or Fashionable Canes and Walking Sticks (www.fashionablecanes.com).

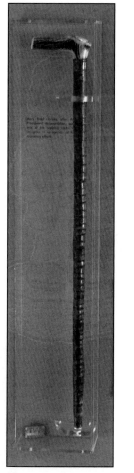

Photo by author, courtesy National Park Service, Frederick Douglass National Historic Site

voting rights, for African Americans became the topic of the hour. As a result, the National Loyalist's Convention was scheduled to be held in Philadelphia during the month of September 1866.

To his surprise and honor, his home city of Rochester, New York, elected Frederick Douglass as its delegate to attend the convention. Douglass prepared for the event and booked passage on a train. En route, however, he was met by other delegates on the train also traveling to the convention. They tried to persuade Douglass to turn back because he was the only black delegate elected. "As a matter of policy or expediency," Douglass replied to them, "you will be wise to let me in." Pressing his point even further, Douglass bravely concluded, "I am bound to go into that convention; not to do so would contradict the principle and practice of my life."

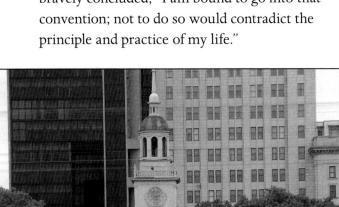

Independence Hall in Philadelphia, Pennsylvania.
Photo by author

A Day in History

Frederick Douglass arrived in Philadelphia. A parade was scheduled to take place before the convention began. Unsure of his reception by the crowd, Douglass made his way to Independence Hall, the site where the parade would start. Two by two, the delegates were supposed to march, but who would march with Douglass?

Douglass was deeply touched when Theodore Tilton, the editor of the largest weekly journal in New York, walked up to him and shook his hand. The warmth of Tilton's hand warmed Douglass's heart. Side-by-side, black and white together, these two delegates joined the parade. Cheers rang out on each street corner they turned. "Hurrah for Douglass!" voices cried. People clapped and cheered as they recognized this great man and American hero who devoted his life to bringing slavery to an end.

And suddenly it happened. Frederick Douglass spotted a familiar face in the crowd. A woman stood at the corner of Ninth and Chestnut Streets. Could it be? It was! It was Amanda Auld Sears, the daughter of his owners from plantation days, Lucretia and Thomas Auld. "I hastily ran to her," Frederick Douglass said, "and expressed my surprise and joy at meeting her. 'But what brought you to Philadelphia at this time?' I asked. She replied, with animated voice and countenance, 'I heard you were to be here, and I came to see you walk in this procession.' The dear lady, with her two children, had been following us for hours."

Meeting his former master's daughter like this was a sign to Douglass that times were indeed changing. After the parade, he attended the convention and spoke out in favor of giving black men the vote. Others opposed his views, but stronger voices agreed with Douglass. The result of the convention was that the issue of suffrage moved forward at an even faster pace than he expected.

Woman's Suffrage Leaders

Frederick Douglass's strong stand caused disagreements among his circle of friends. Leaders of the woman's suffrage movement were disappointed in Douglass's new cause. They felt that women should be given the power to vote before blacks were. Many felt that because white women were more educated than former slaves, they would make better choices at the ballot box.

Frederick Douglass strongly disagreed. He expressed his desire for *all* American citizens to vote, both men and women. He apologized to supporters of women's rights and expressed his sorrow that women didn't yet have the power to vote. However, he argued clearly, "If the Negro knows enough to fight for his country he knows enough to vote; if he knows enough to pay taxes for the support of the government, he knows enough to vote."

He urged women suffragists to wait patiently just a little while longer, for now was the hour of the black man. What use was it for white women to get the power to vote when they would mostly support the vote of their husbands? Giving white women the power to vote would double the strength of the former slaveholder's household as well as the abolitionist household. "No!" Douglass cried. The Civil War would have been fought in vain if the result was that white women received the power to vote. "No!" Douglass insisted. The Civil War was fought for the freedom and rights of former slaves. Now was the black man's hour!

Frederick Douglass's efforts were not in vain. "Unlike the movement for the abolition of slavery," he rejoiced, "the success of the effort for the enfranchisement of the freedmen was not long delayed." In 1870 the Fifteenth Amendment to the Constitution of the United States was ratified and made into law.

> **"The liberties of the American people were dependent upon the ballot-box, the jury-box, and the cartridge-box."**
> **—Frederick Douglass**

Reconstruction

After the Civil War ended slavery, the United States of America entered a span of years known as Reconstruction. Leaders such as Frederick Douglass worked to help newly freed men, women,

"The First Vote" by A. R. Waud. *Courtesy of the Library of Congress, LC-USZ62-19234*

and children transition into their new way of life. Politicians worked in Congress to help the southern states join the nation once again. The constitutions of southern states were rewritten to include black residents as citizens. Former masters were required to hire black workers as laborers rather than rule over them as owners. Military troops were stationed throughout the South for a short time to help establish law and order.

During these years, Frederick Douglass was busy performing his part to help teach fellow citizens how to rebuild their lives. For a short time, he stepped into the role of editor-in-chief with the Washington, DC, newspaper the *New National Era,* before handing over the responsibilities to his sons Lewis and Frederick Jr.

He also developed connections with the Freedmen's Savings and Trust Company, more commonly known as the Freedmen's Bank. For a short time Frederick Douglass was the president of this bank, which had been established to hold the finances and savings of newly freed men and women, especially throughout the southern states.

These were difficult years for Frederick Douglass as well as the rest of the nation. Prejudice ran high. Dishonesty ran rampant. Violence erupted with terrible force against the newly freed. The Ku Klux Klan raged their deadly warfare, and many of the freedmen's rights were snatched away through unfair legalities before they could be enjoyed.

Political unrest boiled throughout the nation as Congress worked to give African American men the power to vote while at the same time rewriting the constitutions of the states throughout the South. Friends urged Frederick Douglass to move south and run for office, but he declined, intent instead on the work he could do as an advocate of the oppressed.

Douglass rejoiced, however, to see African Americans join the lines at the ballot boxes and cast their votes after the Fourteenth and Fifteenth Amendments were passed. For the first time in the nation's history, blacks were voted into the US Congress.

Fire!

In June 1872 Frederick Douglass was away from home when he heard the news. Fire! His home in Rochester, New York, had burned to the ground. Whispers reached his ears that someone started the fire on purpose. Speeding immediately to the scene, Douglass felt as if he were attending a funeral. Anna, along with Rosetta and her husband, had been able to save a few things, but the blaze had been too hot, too quick, and too furious. Gone was a household of precious possessions and years of family mementos. Gone were keepsakes from his trips and dedicated work as an abolitionist. And gone were his issues of his newspapers.

Douglass's heart felt heavy with sadness at the great loss, especially the irreplaceable loss of 12 volumes of his newspaper covering a span of 12 years. Even though one kind friend donated two of the missing volumes to Douglass after the fire, he was never able to replace the other ones.

The first black senator and representatives elected to Congress. Front row (from left to right): Senator Hiram Rhodes Revels of Mississippi, Representatives Benjamin Turner of Alabama, Josiah Walls of Florida, Joseph Hayne Rainey of South Carolina, and Robert Brown Elliott of South Carolina. Back row (from left to right): Representatives Robert DeLarge of South Carolina and Jefferson Long of Georgia. *Courtesy of the Library of Congress, LC-USZC2-2325*

MICROFINANCING

➥ After the Civil War came to an end, Frederick Douglass worked for a short time as the president of the Freedmen's Bank. The principle of this bank was to help people, mostly newly freed slaves, who had little or no money to get a start in the world.

Today, microfinancing, or using small amounts of money to help people living in poverty, is making big news. Opportunities such as microlending operate under a key basic principle: with a small investment of money you can help someone help himself. For example, by loaning $25 to a man or woman in a different country, that person can buy a goat. The goat will supply milk to drink. Its babies can be sold. Some of the money can be used to

pay back the loan. The rest of the money can be used to buy several chickens. Before long, that person's family could have goats, chickens, cows, a new business, and food to eat.

Then you can loan your $25 to a different man or woman and start this amazing success story all over again!

If you would like to participate in a microlending program, check out organizations such as Kiva (www.kiva.org), Microplace (www.microplace.com), and Acción (www.accion.org). Another microfinancing option to help battle poverty is to donate a small gift through an organization such as Heifer International (www.heifer.org).

Frederick and Anna Douglass lived in this house in the heart of Washington, DC, for over five years.
Photo by author

Twelve years of influential work were lost to history. *"If I have at any time said or written that which is worth remembering or repeating,"* he said, *"I must have said such things between the years 1848 and 1860, and my paper was a chronicle of most of what I said during that time."* Some of the great events he had covered in that time span included the Free Soil Convention at Buffalo, the nomination of Martin Van Buren, the Fugitive Slave Law of 1850, the *Dred Scott* decision, the repeal of the Missouri Compromise, the Kansas Nebraska Bill, the Border War in Kansas known as Bleeding Kansas, the John Brown raid upon Harpers Ferry, and the beginning of the Civil War.

Anna and Frederick Douglass took stock of their lives. They weighed important factors regarding the nation's current needs as well as their own personal plans. They made a crucial decision: they decided to move from Rochester, New York, to Washington, DC.

Political Statesman

A grand and influential new career opened for Frederick Douglass. Now living at the nation's capital in Washington, DC, Douglass stepped into his nation's political arena. Never before had African Americans risen to such a position of power and influence, but the times were changing. Black representatives and senators were elected. Frederick Douglass joined the ranks of political leadership in the United States of America.

Four different presidents appointed Frederick Douglass to important government positions. As a loyal advocate of the oppressed, Douglass first and foremost considered civil rights and equality among all peoples as he fulfilled each of his various roles. He traveled to such places as Santo Domingo and Haiti, spending significant time meeting with government officials, key leaders, and important individuals.

Presidents sought out his advice, and Douglass eagerly offered it. Able to evaluate each situation from his unique vantage point, Frederick Douglass's wise words were always valuable. Not one to sway with the tide, Douglass stayed true to his convictions for the personal rights of all mankind whether black or white, man or woman, rich or poor. His voice rang out in these years on behalf of the best interests of his nation and his fellow Americans.

Douglass walked freely and bravely among the leaders of the United States, often in the midst of severe prejudice and outspoken misrepresentation among the press, while always staying in touch with the needs and current situations of the downtrodden and disadvantaged. Frederick Douglass persevered along the path he had chosen, and he stood head and shoulders above the crowds.

Returning to His Roots

At the height of his political influence, Frederick Douglass embarked on a personal journey to revisit his childhood roots. Even though he had traveled far and wide in the years since he

Douglass Inquiring Plantation Owners in Santo Domingo by James E. Taylor.
Courtesy National Park Service, Museum Management Program and Frederick Douglass National Historic Site; FRDO 175, Carol M. Highsmith, photographer, www.cr.nps. gov/museum

From Slave to Statesman

Frederick Douglass achieved landmark success with his presidential appointments and in his political career.

1871 Commissioner to Santo Domingo, appointment by President Grant
1872 Nomination for vice president by Equal Rights Party alongside presidential nominee Victoria Woodhull, but Douglass supported election of President Grant instead
1877 US marshal for the District of Columbia, appointment by President Hayes
1881 Recorder of Deeds for the District of Columbia, appointment by President Garfield
1889 Minister and Consul to Haiti, appointment by President Harrison

Courtesy of the Library of Congress, LC-DIG-cwpbh-05089

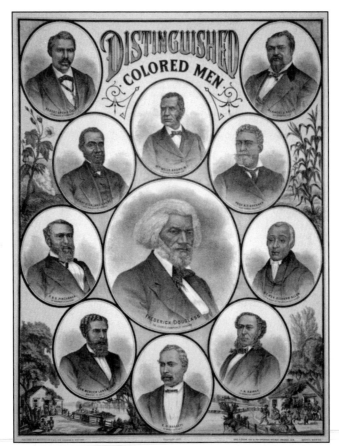

Frederick Douglass led the influential leaders of his day to pave the way for the American civil rights movement.
Courtesy of the Library of Congress, LC-USZC4-1561

Years earlier, in 1848, on the 10th anniversary of his escape, the pangs of separation from his family deeply troubled Frederick Douglass. It was evening, and his household was quiet. Little Rosetta and the rest of his children were sleeping in their warm beds under the safety of their father's roof. The delicious smell of Anna's homemade bread and hearty supper still lingered in the air. Frederick Douglass sat down next to a flickering lamp and took pen and paper in hand.

Heart full, he wrote a letter to his old master and slaveholder, Thomas Auld. In the letter, Douglass implored Auld to send him information about his brother and sisters. He pleaded with Auld to set his grandmother free, if she was still alive, and send her to live with him in Rochester where he could love her and care for her as should be his natural human right. He challenged Auld to step into *his* shoes for a moment and imagine if Douglass held Auld's family in bondage—what would be Auld's thoughts? His feelings? His passions? His pain?

Douglass mailed the letter but received no reply.

At some point, Douglass learned that his sister Eliza had married and been set free in the 1830s when her free husband had purchased her and her children. Eliza and Frederick stayed in contact as much as they could.

For over 40 years, Frederick Douglass searched to find his brother Perry. He sent agents deep into the southern states. It wasn't until after the war ended, however, that the brothers were finally reunited. Perry was in Texas at the time,

escaped from slavery, he never could forget his childhood, living enslaved in Maryland as property of the Auld family.

His heart was still full of sorrow because of his early separation from his family. He missed his beloved grandmother. He missed the natural affections he should have been able to share with his brother and sisters but which slavery denied them. Even though he had been living as a free citizen for many years, laws and slave codes had kept him out of the state of Maryland prior to the Civil War.

still enslaved, when he heard that emancipation had come. Finally learning of Perry's whereabouts, Douglass brought him and his family to Rochester where they settled in a house nearby. The joy in everyone's hearts was beyond what words could describe.

Once the Civil War was over, there were no laws keeping free African Americans out of Maryland; all blacks were forever free. Now Frederick Douglass was a great man, famous on both sides of the Atlantic Ocean, appointed by President Hayes to be US Marshal for the District of Columbia. It was in this position of influence that Frederick Douglass decided to return to Talbot County on Maryland's Eastern Shore. It was a journey long overdue, one that he had yearned to embark on for many years. He decided to go home.

An Unexpected Visit

Frederick Douglass accepted the invitation of his friend Charles Caldwell to visit Talbot County, Maryland, the place Douglass had been born. While there, an unexpected invitation arrived. Captain Thomas Auld, feeble, bedridden, and in his 80s, had heard that Douglass was in the area. Auld's servant met with Douglass and expressed Auld's wishes. Would Douglass come to visit him?

Without hesitation, Frederick Douglass accepted the offer. "Now that slavery was destroyed," Douglass explained, "and the slave and the master stood upon equal ground, I was not only willing to meet him, but was very glad to do so." Even though his memories were full of his old master's harsh and horrific actions as

(left) Historic marker in St. Michaels, Talbot County, Maryland, near the site where Frederick Douglass once lived as a slave and returned years later as a famous statesman.
Photo by author

(right) The Mitchell House in St. Michaels, Maryland, was home to Eliza Bailey Mitchell and her family. Frederick and Eliza stayed in contact as much as their circumstances allowed.
Photo by author

slaveholder, Douglass did not harbor bitterness in his heart. Douglass said, "I regarded him as I did myself, a victim of the circumstances of birth, education, law, and custom. Our courses had been determined for us, not by us."

When Frederick Douglass arrived at the home of William and Louisa Bruff, Auld's son-in-law and daughter, he was greeted graciously and taken to Thomas Auld's bedside. "We addressed each other simultaneously," Douglass remembered. "He calling me 'Marshal Douglass,' and I, as I had always called him, 'Captain Auld.'"

The two men shook hands. Moved by great emotion, tears flowed down Auld's cheeks and Douglass could not find his voice.

When at last both men could speak again, Douglass asked Auld what he thought about his escape from slavery. "He hesitated a moment," Douglass shared, "as if to properly formulate his reply, and said: 'Frederick, I always knew you were too smart to be a slave, and had I been in your place, I should have done as you did.' I said, 'Capt. Auld, I am glad to hear you say this. I did not run away from *you*, but from *slavery*; it was not that I loved Caesar less, but Rome more.'"

The two men talked peacefully together. Auld reassured Douglass that he had taken note of his concern for his grandmother and in her old age had rescued her from poverty to care for her. This brought a measure of comfort to Douglass's heart. After a short time, for Thomas Auld was very weak and sick, the two parted ways. A chapter in the life of Frederick Douglass had drawn to a close. Thomas Auld died soon after that unforgettable day.

> **"The abolition of slavery has not merely emancipated the Negro, but liberated the whites."**
> **—Frederick Douglass**

(left) In 1877 Frederick Douglass visited his old master Thomas Auld here in the home of Auld's daughter in St. Michaels, Maryland. *Photo by author*

(right) In 1878 Douglass stayed at the Brick Hotel in Easton, Maryland, where he received callers in between well-attended speaking engagements. *Photo by author*

Their Native Son

Times had changed the hearts of many, even if not all. Frederick Douglass was deeply glad to see that former slaveholder and former slave could now stand as equals. He hoped every American could experience the healing and peace that he had known.

In 1878 Frederick Douglass returned again to Talbot County, Maryland, for another visit. This time he stayed at the Brick Hotel in Easton, the place next to Law's Tavern, where slave hunters and slave traders used to gather. He remembered that 45 years earlier he had been tied up and locked in the jail across the street for attempting an escape, and slave traders from Law's Tavern had visited him to evaluate his worth.

That was long ago and in a different world, it seemed. Now Douglass was an invited guest at the hotel. As a famous statesman, he spoke at the Talbot County Courthouse next to the jail, where he saw familiar faces of Talbot County officials in his audience. He remembered them well from his days as a slave. While in Easton, he visited local churches and spoke to their congregations.

Talbot County's native son had come home.

Through his efforts as famous abolitionist, brilliant orator, and outspoken newspaper editor, Frederick Douglass had done his part to make such a homecoming possible.

(top left) During his visit to the Maryland's Eastern Shore in 1878, Douglass spoke here to the congregation of the Bethel African Methodist Episcopal (A.M.E.) Church.
Photo by author

(top right) Asbury A.M.E. Church was the second church where Douglass lectured when he visited Easton in Talbot County, Maryland in 1878.
Photo by author

(left) Douglass delivered his "Self-Made Men" speech in 1878 at the Talbot County Courthouse in Easton, Maryland.
Photo by author

"AND THAT GOVERNMENT OF THE PEOPLE, BY THE PEOPLE, FOR THE PEOPLE, SHALL NOT PERISH FROM THE EARTH"

To Honor a Great Man

Frederick Douglass had close friends among well-known white abolitionists and woman's suffrage leaders, as well as leading black men and women of his day. He moved freely among the circles of all his friends, yet many of his biographies showcase only his white contemporaries. Douglass, however, also shared the speaker's platform with, corresponded through letters with, traveled with, attended conventions with, published in his newspapers, and entertained in his own home nearly every black leader, black minister, black educator, and black abolitionist of his day.

Frederick Douglass sculpture.
Photo by author, courtesy of Frederick Douglass–Isaac Myers Maritime Park

Rochester Honors Its Famous Citizen

Frederick Douglass was a great man with great ideals. Several years after he moved to Washington, DC, the city of Rochester commissioned a bust of Douglass's head and shoulders to be carved from marble. Rochester, the city where he had lived for 25 years, decided to honor its most famous citizen.

Frederick Douglass sent a letter expressing his thankfulness for the city's gracious and kind deed. Rochester responded by publishing his letter in a local newspaper along with these words:

Rochester is proud to remember that Frederick Douglass was, for many years, one of her citizens. He who pointed out the house where Douglass lived, hardly exaggerated when he called it the residence of the greatest of our citizens, for Douglass must rank as among the greatest men, not only of this city, but of the nation as well—great in his inspiration, greater in his efforts for humanity—great in the persuasion of his speech, greater in the purpose that informed it.

Along with a marble bust, this statue of Frederick Douglass was also erected in the city of Rochester, New York.
Courtesy of Claire Marziotti

Cedar Hill

In 1878 Frederick Douglass and Anna moved one last time. They purchased a beautiful home named Cedar Hill that sat atop a hillside on a 15-acre estate. Situated in Anacostia, DC, just outside the capital, the Douglasses loved their grand new home. Relaxing in the rockers on their front porch, Frederick and Anna could look to their right over the hills and valleys and see toward Baltimore, the place of Frederick's childhood as a slave and where Frederick and Anna first met. They could also look to the left over the cityscape and see the dome of the nation's capital, the place Douglass now worked as a famous statesman in his appointments by various presidents.

Many happy memories were shared here at Cedar Hill. By now their children were grown

(left) Joseph Douglass, grandson of Frederick Douglass.
Courtesy National Park Service, Museum Management Program and Frederick Douglass National Historic Site; FRDO 3877, Carol M. Highsmith, photographer, www.cr.nps.gov/museum

(right) Cedar Hill, the picturesque home of Frederick Douglass, overlooks the nation's capital.
Photo by author, courtesy National Park Service, Frederick Douglass National Historic Site

and had families of their own. The Douglass grandchildren were always welcome as part of the household when they visited. Frederick and Anna loved their grandchildren and even kept an upstairs bedroom ready for them to spend the night.

Important dignitaries from the nearby capital as well as numerous friends of the family made their way from the crowded city to the peaceful home sitting atop the hill. Anna, who loved to cook, often heard frequent requests for her home-made Maryland beaten biscuits. Tying on her apron, she headed into her kitchen and prepared a delicious home-cooked meal for their guests. By the time their visitors arrived, the house was filled with the savory smells of a tasty dinner and mouth-watering aroma of Anna's signature biscuits.

The Douglass family was very musical. Frederick Douglass's deep voice could be heard singing his favorite songs to entertain their guests. He also enjoyed playing the violin, a love that was picked up by grandson Joseph H. Douglass.

Conversation was lively in the Douglass household, and company was always greeted with open arms. In their personal diaries or letters, various people mentioned the joyous evenings they shared with the Douglass family at Cedar Hill during these years.

SCULPT A STATUE

A famous statue of Frederick Douglass stands in the city of Rochester, New York, to honor one of its greatest citizens.

Materials

* Clean-up supplies such as paper towels and a bucket of water
* Air-dry clay, 2½ pounds
* Paper clip
* Tools for working with clay, such as plastic knife, plastic fork, and plastic spoon
* Rolling pin

➡ For this project, work on a protected surface. Keep paper towels and a bucket of water nearby. Plan to make the statue all at once or the clay might start to dry out.

Divide the clay into three lumps of equal size. Form one lump into a base for the statue. Flatten it into a 1-inch slab and roll it along its edge to form a solid disc.

Write the name "Frederick Douglass" along the front edge of the disc. To write letters in clay, open up a paperclip to make a point, and gently poke little holes to form the shape of each letter. Turn the disc over and write your name and today's date on the bottom. Set this aside.

Roll the second lump of clay into a thick log measuring 6 to 8 inches tall. With your hands, shape one end of the log to form a round ball for the head. The neck can be thick to hold its support. Use a plastic knife to cut the bottom of the log to form the legs. Use the plastic knife to cut two arms.

Shape shoes at the bottom of each leg and position this body onto the base you formed from the first lump. (Follow the directions on the package to join two pieces of clay together. You might need to add a drop or two of water in between the two pieces to help them join permanently.) Shape the body so it stands up on the base, and position the arms to be reaching out at its side.

Use the third lump of clay to add clothes and details to the body. Flatten a thin piece of clay by rolling it with the rolling pin. Cut out a jacket front for one side, fold back the jacket collar, and place it gently on the front left of the statue. Repeat for the front right of the statue. Then cut out a flat rectangle and place it on the back of the statue to complete Douglass's coat.

Roll a 1 x 2-inch flat, thin rectangle and place it on the top of the head to form his hair. A tiny strip of the same thickness can be placed on his chin to form his beard. Use a paper clip to press lightly into the clay to give texture to his hair and beard.

Add details such as his nose, hands, and a tie by pressing tiny shapes of clay to the statue. Draw his eyes and mouth with the point of the paper clip.

Follow the directions on the package of clay to dry the statue.

MARYLAND BEATEN BISCUITS

Anna Douglass was well known as a wonderful cook. One of the recipes her guests requested most often was Maryland beaten biscuits. These round biscuits, crispy on the outside and chewy on the inside, originally came from Maryland's Eastern Shore during plantation days. The dough was placed on a clean tree stump and pounded with the flat side of an ax for half an hour. The more it was pounded, the lighter the biscuits would be.

Ingredients

* 4 cups flour
* Dash of salt
* 1½ tablespoons lard or vegetable shortening
* 1¾ cup water

Materials

* Mixing bowl
* Fork
* Large cutting board
* Meat tenderizer or mallet
* Cookie sheet

Adult supervision required

➡ Place the flour and salt in a mixing bowl and stir them together. Cut in the lard by pressing it into the flour with a fork. Pour in the water and mix together by hand.

Put the lump of dough of a lightly floured cutting board. Be sure to work on a sturdy surface such as a picnic table or sturdy countertop. Hit the dough repeatedly with the flat size of the meat tenderizer for half an hour, folding it over when it gets thin. Take turns with your family or friends.

When you're finished, roll small pieces of dough into 1½-inch balls and place them on a cookie sheet. Prick the top of each ball with a fork. Bake at 425°F for 25 minutes. Makes 18 biscuits.

The kitchen at Cedar Hill.
Photo by author, courtesy National Park Service, Frederick Douglass National Historic Site

The Douglass Children

Frederick and Anna were very proud of their children, who all grew up to become responsible citizens with families of their own. They made sure their children received the best education, even hiring private tutors when public schools did not open their doors to African Americans. Frederick Douglass enlisted them in his newspaper work and involved them in various aspects of his influential political career.

Rosetta, the oldest of their children, married Nathan Sprague and lived with her family in Rochester. When her parents moved to Washington, DC, Rosetta and her family moved as well, settling in the suburbs of the capital where Nathan found work in real estate. Rosetta had a special bond with both of her parents. At times, she helped her father by writing down lectures and editorials that he dictated. Other times, she helped her mother by writing her letters and notes. Rosetta spoke at the Anna Murray Douglass Union of the Woman's Christian Temperance Union (WCTU) in 1900, sharing memories of her childhood along with a special tribute honoring her mother.

After the Civil War, Lewis Douglass was often seen with his father in various political activities at the nation's capital. He married Helen Loguen, daughter of Bishop J. W. Loguen of the A.M.E. Zion Church. President Grant appointed Lewis as a member of the council of the legislature of the District of Columbia. During the administration of President Hayes, Lewis served

Rosetta Douglass Sprague (1839–1906).
Courtesy of Documenting the American South, the University of North Carolina at Chapel Hill Libraries

Lewis H. Douglass (1840–1908).
Courtesy of Documenting the American South, the University of North Carolina at Chapel Hill Libraries

Frederick Douglass Jr. (1842–1892).
Courtesy of Documenting the American South, the University of North Carolina at Chapel Hill Libraries

Charles Remond Douglass (1844–c. 1929).
Courtesy of Documenting the American South, the University of North Carolina at Chapel Hill Libraries

Frederick Douglass spent many hours working here at his desk writing his letters, speeches, and books.
Photo by author, courtesy National Park Service, Frederick Douglass National Historic Site

as assistant marshal of the District of Columbia before settling into a career in real estate.

Frederick Douglass Jr. worked as a recruiting agent during the Civil War to muster black troops. His job took him deep into southern territory to Mississippi and other states. After the war was over, he married Virginia Hewlett. Frederick Jr. served as court bailiff in the District of Columbia.

Charles Douglass returned home from the Civil War and was married in Rochester. He was soon appointed as a clerk in the War Department, where he served with the Freedmen's Bureau. Active in various political and presidential appointments, Charles traveled as a US consul to Santo Domingo. He was involved with the Capital City Guard Corps, the Washington, DC, militia that he commanded as major. His work with the county schools was influential in hiring African Americans as teachers with equal salary benefits.

A Great Storyteller

Never having received one day of formal schooling in his life, Frederick Douglass was still a well-educated man. He was a man of letters and he wrote constantly. For years he wrote newspaper articles, speeches, and letters.

He was also a man of books. He devoured books, both modern and historic as well as classic. He surrounded himself with books in his home. In his personal library at Cedar Hill he filled bookshelves to overflowing. He owned over 2,000 books.

Frederick Douglass was also a great storyteller. He loved to tell stories to guests and family members who visited him in his home. Friends recalled that Douglass rivaled President Lincoln in his ability and love for telling a story. Often, because of the clever wit and jovial spirit Douglass had, his stories made his listeners laugh.

Combining his love for writing, books, and telling stories, Frederick Douglass worked on his autobiography throughout his lifetime. His third autobiography, *Life and Times of Frederick Douglass*, was published in 1881. He continued to update this last biography as the final years of his life unfolded. It was rereleased in various subsequent versions.

Colonel Lloyd's Plantation

Even though Frederick Douglass had returned to the Eastern Shores of Maryland, he had never been back to visit Colonel Lloyd's plantation since the day he sailed away from it when he was about seven years old and was sent to live in Baltimore as a slave for Hugh Auld. Expressing his desire to see the old plantation once again, a friend offered to take Douglass in his small boat, along with several other friends.

Douglass was hesitant, unsure how the descendants of the great Colonel Lloyd would greet him. As their small boat sailed down the river and tied up anchor at the dock, a wide range of emotions flooded Douglass's heart. "From the deck of our vessel," he remembered, "I saw once more the stately chimneys of the grand old mansion which I had last seen from the deck of the *Sally Lloyd* when a boy. I left there as a slave, and returned as a freeman; I left there unknown to the outside world, and returned well known."

Douglass's concerns were soon put to rest. He and his friends received a gracious invitation to come up to the house. The group visited with young Howard Lloyd, the great-grandson of Colonel Edward Lloyd, who escorted them through the estate. A number of the buildings were still the same as when Douglass had lived there.

Together, they walked to the Lloyds' family cemetery and stood under the quiet, towering trees. They meandered through the beautiful gardens. When their tour of the grounds was

LIFE AND TIMES
OF
FREDERICK DOUGLASS
WRITTEN BY HIMSELF.
HIS EARLY LIFE AS A SLAVE, HIS ESCAPE FROM BONDAGE,
AND
HIS COMPLETE HISTORY TO THE PRESENT TIME,
INCLUDING
HIS CONNECTION WITH THE ANTI-SLAVERY MOVEMENT; HIS LABORS IN GREAT BRITAIN
AS WELL AS IN HIS OWN COUNTRY; HIS EXPERIENCE IN THE CONDUCT OF AN
INFLUENTIAL NEWSPAPER; HIS CONNECTION WITH THE UNDERGROUND RAILROAD;
HIS RELATIONS WITH JOHN BROWN AND THE HARPER'S FERRY RAID; HIS
RECRUITING THE 54TH AND 55TH COLORED REGIMENTS; HIS INTER-
VIEWS WITH PRESIDENTS LINCOLN AND JOHNSON; HIS APPOINTMENT
BY GEN. GRANT TO ACCOMPANY THE SANTO DOMINGO COMMISSION—
ALSO TO A SEAT IN THE COUNCIL OF THE DISTRICT OF COLUMBIA;
HIS APPOINTMENT AS UNITED STATES MARSHAL BY PRESIDENT
R. B. HAYES; ALSO HIS APPOINTMENT TO BE RECORDER OF
DEEDS IN WASHINGTON BY PRESIDENT J. A. GARFIELD;
WITH MANY OTHER INTERESTING AND IMPORTANT
EVENTS OF HIS MOST EVENTFUL LIFE;
WITH
AN INTRODUCTION BY MR. GEORGE L. RUFFIN,
OF BOSTON.
New Revised Edition.
BOSTON:
DE WOLFE & FISKE CO.

During his lifetime, Frederick Douglass wrote three autobiographies, including *Narrative of the Life of Frederick Douglass, My Bondage and My Freedom,* and this final one, *Life and Times of Frederick Douglass. Courtesy of Documenting the American South, the University of North Carolina at Chapel Hill Libraries*

In 1881 Frederick Douglass visited the great house at Colonel Lloyd's plantation. *Photo by author, courtesy of Frederick Douglass–Isaac Myers Maritime Park*

who had been enslaved on that very plantation and whom Douglass had known when he was a child.

It was a very emotional experience for Douglass. He shared, "That I was deeply moved and greatly affected by it can be easily imagined." He realized that a visit such as this was "one which could happen to but few men, and only once in the life time of any." Returning with his friends to the dock, they climbed aboard their ship and turned for home.

A Great Loss

In August 1882 the Douglass household experienced a great loss. Beloved wife, mother, and grandmother Anna Murray Douglass passed away. In September Frederick and Anna would have been married for 44 years.

Frederick grieved for the loss of Anna. She had befriended him and invited him to join her circle of free blacks in Baltimore while he was still a slave. She had made arrangements and helped plan his escape to freedom. In their early years of marriage, they had shared the joys of settling into their new home together and raising a family. A hard worker with a head for finances, Anna had provided the support and financial stability their family needed through hard economic times and limited salaries generated from Frederick's work as an abolitionist. When he was forced to flee abroad in danger of his life, Anna had kept the home fires burning and the family knit closely together. A devout abolitionist herself,

complete, Douglass and his companions were invited to sit on the grand veranda of the great house and enjoy the stately view.

After their short rest, Howard Lloyd invited them inside the house, where they were offered refreshments in the dining room. Once outside again, Douglass was greeted by various people who stopped by because they heard he was visiting. A number of them were children of people

Anna had been influential and well known among her friends in her antislavery circles.

Now she was gone.

She would be sorely missed.

A New Season

Time marched on as Frederick Douglass dealt with his grief and sorrow. As days turned into months and then a full year went by, however, Douglass was lonely. His grand house on Cedar Hill felt empty. He decided to marry again.

As the Recorder of Deeds for the District of Columbia, Frederick Douglass had hired a clerk to help him with the paperwork. Helen Pitts supported woman's suffrage and believed in equality of the races. Her ancestors had arrived in America on the *Mayflower*, and she came from a prestigious family. She was 45.

In 1884 Frederick and Helen were married. Reverend Francis Grimké, husband of Charlotte Forten Grimké, performed the wedding ceremony. With their similar political beliefs and interests, Frederick and Helen had many things in common. However, because Frederick was black and Helen was white, the marriage caused strong objections from different people.

As usual, these protests did not sway Frederick Douglass's firm convictions in equal rights. He responded to public opinion by stating that when he married a woman the same color as his mother, nobody objected, but now that he married a woman the same color as his father, many people protested.

(left) Silver tea set in the Douglass home at Cedar Hill.
Photo by author, courtesy National Park Service, Frederick Douglass National Historic Site

(right) Helen Pitts Douglass, second wife of Frederick Douglass.
Courtesy National Park Service, Museum Management Program and Frederick Douglass National Historic Site; FRDO 318, Carol M. Highsmith, photographer, www.cr.nps.gov/museum

Not everyone protested, however. For those who knew Frederick Douglass and the principles he lived for, they understood that race or skin color made no difference to this great man. It was the quality and character of a person that mattered to him. He chose to marry his new wife because he loved her.

The house at Cedar Hill once more rang out with the voices of happy guests and welcome visitors. The back lawn behind the house was used as a croquet court. Numerous delightful hours were spent with friends and family playing lively games of croquet, with Frederick Douglass often winning many of the matches himself.

Helen and Frederick also shared a love for music. She played the piano and often accompanied him as he played the violin. The sweet melodies they enjoyed together filled the home at Cedar Hill with light and happiness once again.

The Trip of a Lifetime

From September 1886 to August 1887, Frederick and Helen Douglass embarked on the trip of a lifetime. They spent that year touring Europe. The couple started in England to visit Douglass's old friends from the years he spent in exile on that country's friendly shores.

As Frederick and Helen traveled by train from London to Paris and on to Rome, they enjoyed the beautiful countryside, the ancient cities, and the friendly people. They stopped at many historic towns and museums along the way. They visited formidable castles, toured quaint villages, and explored beautiful gardens.

Throughout his trip, Douglass felt an amazing variety of emotions. When they toured the old castles and peered into the dark recesses of torture chambers, he felt sad. He remembered his own experiences as a slave and questioned how any person could treat a fellow human being so. When he walked through a Roman amphitheater where years ago men fought with wild beasts before wildly cheering crowds, Douglass remembered his nation's sorrowful history of slavery. He wondered sadly what it was in the human heart that could find amusement in such terrible sports.

When they stood on the shore and smelled the salty waters of the Mediterranean Sea, Douglass took a deep breath and marveled that the air he breathed wafted over to them from

The Douglass's piano and violin in their home at Cedar Hill.
Photo by author, courtesy National Park Service, Frederick Douglass National Historic Site

Africa's golden shores. And when they had traveled down to the land of the pharaohs, where he saw his first camel, groaning under the strain of its heavy burden, Douglass said, "I have large sympathy with all burden-bearers, whether they be men or beasts. . . . I had at the moment much the same feeling as when I first saw a gang of slaves chained together and shipped to a foreign market."

Several highlights of the trip were treasured by Frederick Douglass. He saw many famous items in places such as the Museum of Genoa in Italy. He recalled, however, "that the one that touched me most was the violin that had belonged to and been played upon by Paganini, the greatest musical genius of his time." He could scarcely pull himself away.

When Douglass visited Rome, it was hard for him to describe the feelings he experienced knowing that he was walking in the footsteps of Paul from the Bible. Douglass said, "It was something to feel ourselves standing where this brave man stood, looking on the place where he lived, and walking on the same Appian Way where he walked."

In Egypt, the land of the Nile, Douglass observed that "nothing grows old here but time, and that lives on forever." He decided to climb to the top of the Great Pyramid and with typical humor recalled that he made the climb with some difficulty. "I had two Arabs before me pulling, and two at my back pushing, but the main work I had to do myself." As he stood on the top of the pyramid, looking out over the stark and

beautiful desert where stood the Sphinx, the other pyramids, and the sites of ancient cities now vanished in the shifting sands of time, he marveled that "there are stirred in the one who beholds it for the first time thoughts and feelings never thought and felt before."

Finally, at year's end, his grand and glorious trip came to an end. It was time to return home. With Helen's hand in his, they headed back to Cedar Hill.

> "After my life of hardships in slavery and of conflict with race and color prejudice and proscription at home, there was left to me a space in life when I could and did walk the world unquestioned, a man among men."
> —Frederick Douglass

The Darkest Hour

If the years of slavery were the nation's most sorrowful hour and the years of the Civil War the nation's bloodiest hour, the years that followed the war became America's darkest hour. All the freedoms, all the rights, all the humanity for an oppressed race that men had died for on the battlefield were swept away, almost before they had time to take root.

Frederick Douglass watched the tide of events with a heart that was filled with sorrow, yet ever with hope. As always, he lifted his voice and let it be heard.

Early in these years as the US marshal of the District of Columbia, Douglass felt it a great honor when he escorted both the outgoing and incoming president during the ceremonies conducted for James Garfield's inauguration into office. He said, "I deemed the event highly important as a new circumstance in my career, as a new recognition of my class, and as a new step in the progress of the nation."

Hope filled Douglass's heart when President Garfield spoke privately with Douglass for advice

In his position as US marshal, Frederick Douglass escorted newly elected President Garfield during his inauguration ceremony. *Courtesy of Documenting the American South, the University of North Carolina at Chapel Hill Libraries*

on using African Americans as statesmen. Yet this same hope was dashed to the ground when President Garfield was assassinated. "His death," lamented Douglass, "appeared to me as among the gloomiest calamities that could have come to my people."

For a short time after the war, a period of Reconstruction worked in favor of equal rights throughout the nation. But as those years drew to an end, a period of mob violence and terror took its place. Frederick Douglass observed these terrible events with a sad and heavy heart. He said, "The country had not quite survived the effects and influence of its great war for existence. The serpent had been wounded but not killed."

> **"My cause first, midst, last, and always, whether in office or out of office, was and is that of the black man—not because he is black, but because he is a man, and a man subjected in this country to peculiar wrongs and hardships." —Frederick Douglass**

In this the nation's darkest hour Frederick Douglass remained at his post, letting his voice be heard through the influential government positions he held. He spoke at key meetings, wrote letters of influence, and worked hard to fight for civil rights.

Appointment to Haiti

In 1881 Frederick Douglass was appointed by President Benjamin Harrison to be the minister resident and consul general to Haiti. As usual, Douglass viewed his role in Haiti from a unique perspective. He understood the concerns the small, impoverished nation of Haiti had when approached by strong-arm tactics from the United States to establish a navy base on its shores. Douglass recognized the prejudice of Americans who met with the government leaders in Haiti, trying to arrange commerce deals and political deals to their own advantage.

In his appointed position, Douglass stayed true to his moral convictions, unswayed by politics, public opinion, or bad press. He knew how to deal with lies, scandals, and prejudice. He valued the people of Haiti and their leaders, many of them former slaves or descendants of slaves. And in 1892 when the government of Haiti appointed him to be their representative as the commissioner of the Haitian exhibit at the World's Columbian Exhibition in Chicago, Frederick Douglass considered it a great honor.

His Final Stand

By the late 1800s mob violence ravaged the South, establishing a reign of terror against blacks. Lynch law, where southern citizens took matters in their own hands and lynched anyone they chose, was responsible for the murders of scores of innocent African Americans. Throughout the

Frederick Douglass at his desk in Haiti.
Courtesy National Park Service, Museum Management Program and Frederick Douglass National Historic Site; FRDO 3899, Carol M. Highsmith, photographer, www.cr.nps.gov/museum

Charles Burleigh Purvis (1842-1929)

Charles Burleigh Purvis served as a surgeon during the Civil War. After the war, he was appointed as the head of Freedmen's Hospital in Washington, DC, becoming the first African American to hold such a position. Son of famous abolitionists Robert and Harriet Forten Purvis, Charles helped mend a division between his father and Frederick Douglass over their different views on how to bring slavery to an end.

Courtesy of Documenting the American South, the University of North Carolina at Chapel Hill Libraries

BANANA LEAF CARD

A traditional craft in Haiti uses banana leaves to create designs on cards.

Materials

* Banana leaves (can be found in the frozen section of most Asian markets)
* Cardstock or sturdy paper, 8½ x 11 inches
* Pencil
* Scissors
* Craft glue

➡ Dry the banana leaves outside in the sun. Fold the piece of cardstock or sturdy paper in half to make a card. On the front of the card, use a pencil to draw a design. You can draw a traditional design from Haiti such as a basket or a palm tree, or you can draw any design you choose.

Cut the banana leaves into small pieces and glue the pieces onto the card to fill in the design in an interesting way. To make a palm tree, cut a flat part of a dried banana leaf into small triangles and glue these close together to form the trunk of the palm tree. Then cut a flat part of the banana leaf into leaf-shaped pieces and glue these at the top of the tree to form the palm fronds.

North, many people joined in the tide of opinion against former slaves, believing the lies painted by the press and southern government leaders who declared blacks were unfit for citizenship, unworthy of rights afforded to American citizens, and unequipped to vote.

The black lion, as Frederick Douglass was now known, shook his mane in anger and roared as never before. Douglass declared emancipation had become a fraud! Where was justice? Where was trial by jury and the protection of the Constitution? Where was government of the people, by the people, and for the people? Let the law be obeyed, Douglass demanded, and the nation's problem would right itself.

Point by point, example by example, and speech by speech, Frederick Douglass made the truth be known. The newspapers, southern legislatures, and northern sentiments endorsed mob violence as an excuse to take away the power of the black vote. Douglass recognized the slanderous tactics. His speeches during these years were so brilliant that countless copies were printed and distributed throughout the South. Hope was restored once again.

Now in the twilight of his years, Douglass heard a new voice rise up in America to carry the torch. Ida B. Wells caught the fire that burned brightly in the heart of Frederick Douglass. She made it her personal cause to expose the horrible truth about the epidemic of lynchings that spread its sickness throughout America.

Douglass and Wells corresponded often. They wrote a pamphlet together about racism that was given out to visitors to the World's Columbian Exposition in Chicago. The day would come, Douglass believed, when the United States would see its African American citizens enjoying the full freedoms to which they were entitled. With new voices and a new generation to lead the fight for civil rights, he was sure of it.

Saying Good-bye

On February 20, 1895, Frederick Douglass attended the Women's Council, a women's rights organization, in Washington, DC. When the meeting adjourned, he returned to his house at Cedar Hill where he had dinner with Helen. Later that evening, he collapsed in his home from a heart attack and died.

The nation mourned.

His wife, children, and grandchildren held a private service at Cedar Hill to give a tender good-bye.

Ida B. Wells-Barnett (1862-1931)

A journalist from Memphis, Tennessee, Ida B. Wells made it her personal crusade to let America know about the horrible lynchings and mob violence that were terrorizing the nation. In 1893 Frederick Douglass collaborated with Wells to write a pamphlet that explained how racism excluded most blacks from participating in the World's Columbian Exposition in Chicago.

Courtesy of the Library of Congress,
LC-USZ62-107756

Paul Laurence Dunbar (1872-1906)

As a young poet, Paul Laurence Dunbar traveled to Chicago and found work at the World's Columbian Exposition. He was appointed clerk to Frederick Douglass. After Douglass lectured at the fair, Dunbar stepped forward to the speaker's platform and read aloud "The Colored Soldiers," his stirring poem in honor of black troops who fought during the Civil War. Douglass warmly praised his skills. Later, upon hearing of Douglass's death, Dunbar wrote a poem in honor of this great man.

A funeral service was held in the Metropolitan A.M.E. Church in Washington, DC. Thousands of mourners passed by the casket in double lines. Standing guard were members of the Sons of Veterans, descendants of black troops who fought in America's wars. Important political leaders from the nation's capital attended the funeral service. Many speeches and touching stories were shared. Longtime friend and woman's suffrage leader Susan B. Anthony rose to read a letter from Elizabeth Cady Stanton written for the service. Pallbearers included former senator B. H. Bruce, P. B. S. Pinchback, and Dr. Charles Burleigh Purvis. Local businesses and schools closed. Newspapers on both sides of the Atlantic Ocean carried the news that one of the greatest men in history had left his footsteps forever in the hallmarks of time.

> "Contemplating my life as a whole, I have to say that, although it has at times been dark and stormy, and I have met with hardships from which other men have been exempted, yet my life has in many respects been remarkably full of sunshine and joy." —Frederick Douglass

(left) The Douglass family pew at the Metropolitan A.M.E. Church in Washington, DC.
Photo by author

(right) Metropolitan A.M.E. Church in Washington, DC. Douglass gave his last speech here on January 9, 1894, called the "Lessons of the Hour." At the event, former Senator Blanche K. Bruce introduced the great orator.
Photo by author

After the services in Washington, DC, the casket was transported by train to Rochester, New York. Crowds lined the streets on that cold winter's day. The 54th Massachusetts Band played to honor the nation's great hero. The casket was put on view at city hall, where thousands stood in line to pay their last respects. Even more dignitaries gathered at Central Church for the funeral service. Family and friends also attended this service before bringing the casket to its final resting place in Mount Hope Cemetery. Other memorial services were held throughout the city.

In the years following the death of Frederick Douglass, his widow Helen Pitts Douglass created a memorial at Cedar Hill. His books, papers, and personal possessions were carefully preserved. The house then came under the care of the National Association of Colored Women's Clubs and eventually the National Park Service.

(left) Funeral procession for Frederick Douglass in Rochester, New York. *From the collection of the Rochester Public Library Local History Division*

(below left) Many famous men and women gathered to honor the life of Frederick Douglass at Central Church in Rochester, New York. *From the collection of the Rochester Public Library Local History Division*

(below right) Gravesite of Frederick Douglass in Mount Hope Cemetery, Rochester, New York. *Courtesy of Claire Marziotti*

131

AFTERWORD

A Great Man Among Men

Frederick Douglass was a man of decisions. As a child, he made the decision to learn to read and write because he realized literacy was the path to freedom. When he was a young man, he decided to take freedom into his own hands and escape from slavery. As an abolitionist, he decided to publish his personal story in a book, even though he knew it would endanger his life. And when he had the choice to live in England enjoying peace and equality, he decided to return home to the United States and fight for the freedoms of his people.

Frederick Douglass was a man of principle. He believed in equal rights. Advocate of the oppressed, he worked tirelessly to persuade his fellow Americans to treat each other with decency and respect in all situations. His brilliant speeches, powerful articles, influential books, and decisive actions spurred others to uphold the rights and freedoms outlined in the Constitution as the finest principles Americans could choose to follow.

Frederick Douglass was a man of action. He was the forerunner of the American civil rights movement. Everywhere he went he stepped forward as an equal whether it was in a railroad car, a restaurant, a speaker's platform, a hotel, or the capital of the United States. He instigated the first sit-ins, first freedom rides, first protest marches, and first attempts at integration many regions of the country had ever seen. He inspired others to take a stand in support of equal rights.

Frederick Douglass was a great man among men. A true American hero, his life was a testimony to the power and purpose one individual can pursue to change the world.

Frederick Douglass (1817/1818–1895)

FREDERICK DOUGLASS
by Paul Laurence Dunbar
(Selected stanzas)

A hush is over all the teeming lists,
And there is pause, a breath-space in the strife;
A spirit brave has passed beyond the mists
And vapors that obscure the sun of life.
And Ethiopia, with bosom torn,
Laments the passing of her noblest born.

The place and cause that first aroused his might
Still proved its pow'r until his latest day.
In Freedom's lists and for the aid of Right
Still in the foremost rank he waged the fray;
Wrong lived; His occupation was not gone.
He died in action with his armor on!

We weep for him, but we have touched his hand,
And felt the magic of his presence nigh,
The current that he sent thro' out the land,
The kindling spirit of his battle-cry
O'er all that holds us we shall triumph yet
And place our banner where his hopes were set!

Oh, Douglass, thou hast passed beyond the shore,
But still thy voice is ringing o'er the gale!
Thou 'st taught thy race how high her hopes may soar
And bade her seek the heights, nor faint, nor fail.
She will not fail, she heeds thy stirring cry,
She knows thy guardian spirit will be nigh,
And rising from beneath the chast'ning rod,
She stretches out her bleeding hands to God!

Courtesy of Documenting the American South, the
University of North Carolina at Chapel Hill Libraries

~Resources~

Frederick Douglass for Kids

www.FrederickDouglass.wordpress.com

This is the official site for the book *Frederick Douglass for Kids*. Read Douglass's manumission papers that showed he had purchased his freedom. Learn more about the Latimer case. Read biographies of well-known men and women Douglass associated with and knew. Download a free teacher's guide with reproducible worksheets for classroom use.

Frederick Douglass National Historic Site: Virtual Museum Exhibit

www.cr.nps.gov/museum/exhibits/douglass/

On this site, view photographs of the Douglass home at Cedar Hill. You'll see personal items, favorite possessions, and household accessories used and owned by Frederick Douglass and his family.

Frederick Douglass National Historic Site

www.nps.gov/frdo/index.htm

See what's happening for teachers, kids, and visitors at this site hosted by the National Park Service. A history of Cedar Hill, a list of books Douglass owned, and diaries of Frederick and Helen Pitts Douglass can be viewed.

The Frederick Douglass Papers at the Library of Congress

http://memory.loc.gov/ammem/doughtml/doughome.html

View a detailed time line of Frederick Douglass's life as well as his family tree at this interesting site. You can also find many speeches, letters, and documents to read, some in Douglass's own handwriting.

Many Roads to Freedom: Abolitionism and the Civil War in Rochester

www.libraryweb.org/rochimag/roads/home.htm

Visit this site to learn more about the city where Frederick Douglass lived while he published his newspaper, the *North Star*. See photographs of his abolitionist friends, learn about his branch of the Underground Railroad, and read scrapbooks with newspaper clippings about his funeral.

Places to Visit

Frederick Douglass Driving Tour of Talbot County, Maryland

Take this driving tour to visit the Eastern Shore of Maryland and see the location of Frederick Douglass's birthplace as well as key sites from his childhood as a slave.

A map is available from the Historical Society of Talbot County at www. hstc.org or call (410) 822-0773.

Frederick Douglass-Isaac Myers Maritime Park

1417 Thames Street

Baltimore, Maryland 21231

www.douglassmyers.org

Learn more about Frederick Douglass's life working in Baltimore in the shipyards. Watch a movie about the maritime industry, see a copy of the *Columbian Orator*, and practice caulking a ship. Guided and school group tours are available.

New Bedford Whaling National Historical Park

33 William Street

New Bedford, Massachusetts 02740

www.nps.gov/nebe/index.htm

Learn about the Underground Railroad in New Bedford. Visit Frederick Douglass's first house as a fugitive. Discover a fuller history of the 54th Massachusetts Volunteers in the Civil War. Explore the visitor's center and local whaling museums, and take the walking tour.

Cedar Hill at the Frederick Douglass National Historic Site

1411 W Street SE

Washington, DC 20020

www.nps.gov/frdo/planyourvisit/index.htm

Enjoy a ranger-led walking tour through the beautiful grounds of Cedar Hill, the home of Frederick Douglass near Washington, DC. Stop in the visitor center to see the cane Lincoln's widow presented to Douglass.

Books to Read

* for younger readers

Collier, James Lincoln. *The Frederick Douglass You Never Knew*. New York: Children's Press, 2003.

Davidson, Margaret. *Frederick Douglass Fights for Freedom*. New York: Scholastic, 1968.

Douglass, Frederick. *My Bondage and My Freedom*. New York: Barnes and Noble Classics, 2005.

Douglass, Frederick. *Narrative of the Life of Frederick Douglass, An American Slave, Written By Himself*. New York: W.W. Norton & Company, 1997.

McKissack, Patricia and Fredrick. *Frederick Douglass: The Black Lion*. Chicago: Children's Press, 1987.

* McKissack, Patricia and Fredrick. *Frederick Douglass: Leader Against Slavery*. Berkeley Heights, New Jersey: Enslow Publishers, Inc., 2002.

McLoone, Margo. *Frederick Douglass: A Photo-Illustrated Biography*. Mankato, Minnesota: Capstone Press, 1997.

* Miller, Barbara Kiely. *Frederick Douglass: Great Americans*. Pleasantville, New York: Gareth Stevens, 2008.

Russell, Sharman Apt. *Frederick Douglass: Abolitionist Editor*. Philadelphia: Chelsea House Publishers, 2005.

Sanders, Jeff and Nancy I. Sanders. *Readers Theatre for African American History*. Santa Barbara, CA: Libraries Unlimited, 2008.

Sanders, Nancy I. *A Kid's Guide to African American History*. Chicago: Chicago Review Press, 2007.

Sanders, Nancy I. *America's Black Founders*. Chicago: Chicago Review Press, 2010.

Sanders, Nancy I. *Black Abolitionists (Perspectives on History)*. Carlisle, Massachusetts: History Compass, 2011.

* Sanders, Nancy I. *D is for Drinking Gourd: An African American Alphabet*. Chelsea, MI: Sleeping Bear Press, 2007.

* Spengler, Kremena. *Frederick Douglass: Voice for Freedom*. Mankato, Minnesota: Capstone Press, 2006.

~Index~

978-1-55652-811-8
$16.95 (CAN $18.95)

America's Black Founders

Revolutionary Heroes & Early Leaders with 21 Activities

Nancy I. Sanders

History books are replete with heroic stories of Washington, Jefferson, and Adams, but what of Allen, Russwurm, and Hawley? *America's Black Founders* celebrates the lesser known but significant lives and contributions of our nation's early African American leaders. Many know that the Revolutionary War's first martyr, Crispus Attucks, a dockworker of African descent, was killed at the Boston Massacre. But far fewer know that the final conflict of the war, the Battle of Yorktown, was hastened to a conclusion by James Armistead Lafayette, a slave and spy who reported the battle plans of General Cornwallis to George Washington.

Author Nancy I. Sanders weaves the histories of dozens of men and women—soldiers, sailors, ministers, poets, merchants, doctors, and other community leaders—who have earned proper recognition among the founders of the United States of America. To get a better sense of what these individuals accomplished and the times in which they lived, readers will celebrate Constitution Day, cook colonial foods, publish a newspaper, petition their government, and more. This valuable resource also includes a time line of significant events, a list of historic sites to visit or explore online, and web resources for further study.

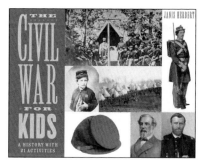

978-1-55652-355-7
$16.95 (CAN $18.95)

Civil War for Kids
A History with 21 Activities

Janis Herbert

"This book provides a look at the Civil War and its leaders and includes activities such as battle reenactments and recipes for soldiers' rations. . . . Ideal for classrooms." —*School Library Journal*

History explodes in this activity guide spanning the turmoil preceding secession, the first shots fired at Fort Sumter, the fierce battles on land and sea, and finally the Confederate surrender at Appomattox. Making butternut dye for a Rebel uniform, learning drills and signals with flags, decoding wigwag, baking hardtack, reenacting battles, and making a medicine kit bring this pivotal period in our nation's history to life. Fascinating sidebars tell of slaves escaping on the Underground Railroad, the adventures of nine-year-old drummer boy Johnny Clem, animal mascots who traveled with the troops, and friendships between enemies. The resource section includes short biographies of important figures from both sides of the war, listings of Civil War sites across the country, pertinent websites, glossary, and an index.

Available at your favorite bookstore, by calling (800) 888-4741, or at www.chicagoreviewpress.com

CHICAGO REVIEW PRESS

978-1-55652-554-4
$16.95 (CAN $18.95)

The Underground Railroad for Kids
From Slavery to Freedom with 21 Activities

Mary Kay Carson

"Densely packed with information." —*School Library Journal*

"Vibrant presentation of inherently action-packed subject matter is reason enough for purchase."
—*Booklist*

"Carson's well-written text gives the background of the movement that led to freedom for thousands of African Americans." —*The Miami Herald*

"A complete historical overview of this dark period in American history." —*Peoria Journal Star*

"Offers children a way to understand the difficult topic of slavery." —*Learning Magazine*

978-1-55652-370-0
$16.95 (CAN $18.95)

The Civil Rights Movement for Kids
A History with 21 Activities

Mary C. Turck

"Pertinent, refreshing, and a true pleasure to read. It is wonderful to see such a comprehensive guide to civil rights education for young people. I am gratified to know that such a meaningful and intensive way to study these important issues is available to families."

—Kweisi Mfume, president, NAACP

"This is a much-needed work that should be in every school and public library, as well as in the home. It is imperative that our youth of today know the history of those who made civil rights their life work and, more importantly, those whose lives were sacrificed so all of mankind could someday enjoy 'life, liberty, and the pursuit of happiness . . .' for which this country stands."

—Myrlie Evers-Williams, chairman emeritus, NAACP

"Well-written and detailed book." —*OC Family*

Available at your favorite bookstore, by calling (800) 888-4741, or at www.chicagoreviewpress.com

CHICAGO REVIEW PRESS